MICHIGAN STATE

DAILY DEVOTIONS FOR DIE-HARD FANS

SPARTANS

MICHIGAN STATE

Daily Devotions for Die-Hard Fans: Michigan State Spartans
© 2017 Ed McMinn
Extra Point Publishers; P.O. Box 871; Perry GA 31069

Unless otherwise noted, scripture quotations are taken from the *Holy Bible, New International Version*. Copyright © 1973, 1978, 1984, by the International Bible Society. Used by permission of Zondervan.

Cover design by John Powell and Slynn McMinn
Interior design by Slynn McMinn

Visit us at die-hardfans.com.

SPARTANS

Daily Devotions for Die-Hard Fans
Available Titles

ACC

Clemson Tigers
Duke Blue Devils
FSU Seminoles
Georgia Tech Yellow Jackets
North Carolina Tar Heels
NC State Wolfpack
Notre Dame Fighting Irish
Virginia Cavaliers
Virginia Tech Hokies

BIG 10

Michigan Wolverines
Michigan State Spartans
Nebraska Cornhuskers
Ohio State Buckeyes
Penn State Nittany Lions

BIG 12

Baylor Bears
Oklahoma Sooners
Oklahoma State Cowboys
TCU Horned Frogs
Texas Longhorns
Texas Tech Red Raiders
West Virginia Mountaineers

SEC

Alabama Crimson Tide
MORE Alabama Crimson Tide
Arkansas Razorbacks
Auburn Tigers
MORE Auburn Tigers
Florida Gators
Georgia Bulldogs
MORE Georgia Bulldogs
Kentucky Wildcats
LSU Tigers
Mississippi State Bulldogs
Missouri Tigers
Ole Miss Rebels
South Carolina Gamecocks
MORE South Carolina Gamecocks
Texas A&M Aggies
Tennessee Volunteers

and *NASCAR*

Daily Devotions for Die-Hard Kids
Available Titles
Alabama, Auburn, Baylor, Georgia, LSU
Miss. State, Ole Miss, Texas, Texas A&M

---

die-hardfans.com

MICHIGAN STATE

DAILY DEVOTIONS FOR DIE-HARD FANS

SPARTANS

IN THE BEGINNING

Read Genesis 1; 2:1-3.

"God saw all that he had made, and it was very good" (v. 1:31).

Football at what was to become Michigan State University faced an uncertain future until the rather unusual decision was made to hire a minister to coach the team.

The first-ever football game at what was then State Agricultural College was a 10-0 defeat of Lansing High School on Sept. 26, 1896. The team had no coach, but left end Scott Redfern served as the squad's manager. Football was late coming to the school because of the intransigence of the faculty and administration. Virtually to a man, they believed all competitive sports were "frivolous, of doubtful morality, and not to be compared to farm work as healthful exercise."

But pressure grew for State to field a team. On April 8, 1895, the state board legitimized intercollegiate athletic competition at the school, and the 1896 season followed. The team went 1-3 in its maiden season, losing twice to Kalamazoo and once to Alma.

Immediately, though, the school faculty launched an effort to abolish football. Fortunately for the institute's athletic history, Jonathan L. Snyder took office as the school's president in 1896. He had played college athletics and was an avid fan. Joining in the effort to establish a true football program was L. Whitney Watkins, a young alumnus who had played baseball and had been the school's lightweight boxing champion.

In 1899, Watkins took the fight to the state board to hire a paid football coach after the team had been coached in 1897 and 1898 by Henry Keep, an engineering student. The board adamantly refused until Snyder came up with a brilliant compromise that rescued football and forever changed the school's athletic history. He proposed the hiring of The Rev. Charles O. Bemies to coach all sports and assume leadership in chapel each morning.

Perhaps reluctantly, the board went along; football at Michigan State University had officially been sanctioned.

Beginnings are important, but what we make of them is even more important. Consider, for example, just how far the Michigan State football program has come since that first season in 1896.

Every morning, you get a gift from God: a new beginning. God hands to you as an expression of divine love a new day full of promise and the chance to right the wrongs in your life. You can use the day to pay a debt, start a new relationship, replace a burned-out light bulb, tell your family you love them, chase a dream, solve a nagging problem . . . or not.

God simply provides the gift. How you use it is up to you. People often talk wistfully about starting over or making a new beginning. God gives you the chance with the dawning of every new day. You have the chance today to make things right — and that includes your relationship with God.

If we must have football, I want the kind that wins.
— School President Jonathan L. Snyder, lending his support to football

Every day is not just a dawn; it is a precious
chance to start over or begin anew.

DAY 2

IN THE BAD TIMES

Read Philippians 1:3-14.

"What has happened to me has really served to advance the gospel. . . . Because of my chains, most of the brothers in the Lord have been encouraged to speak the word of God more courageously and fearlessly" (vv. 12, 14).

Gerald Holmes had a bad two weeks that ended with some good times on the football field.

After a 2015 sophomore season that saw him finish second on the team in rushing, Holmes entered 2016 preseason practice "as one of the starting running backs," according to the Spartans' website. Thus, his disappointment ran deep when he didn't get into the backfield in the 28-13 defeat of Furman in the season opener. He saw only some special teams play.

"It was tough," Holmes admitted. "I felt like I came off a good year last year. So coming in and not really playing, it kind of hit me."

Dashed expectations were bad enough for Holmes, but it got worse over the next two weeks. On Friday, Sept. 17, the day before the second game of the season, against Notre Dame, Holmes' grandmother died. He learned about it during a team meeting that day and fled the room in tears.

After he composed himself, Holmes returned to the meeting and talked to his teammates. He told them that despite the loss and the heartache, he would play Saturday and use his grandmother's death as his motivation.

Head coach Mark Dantonio told Holmes to be ready, and sure enough, his number was called. He ran for a game-high 100 yards and two touchdowns as the Spartans beat Notre Dame 36-28.

The highlight of Holmes' game came late in third quarter when he followed fullback Prescott Line into a hole the line opened up. "Christmas," he thought when he saw the open space before him.

Holmes blasted through the hole and ran 73 yards to the end zone to cinch the win. The good times were back.

Loved ones like your grandmother die. Your company downsizes and you lose your job. Your biopsy looks suspicious. Hard, sometimes tragic times are as much a part of life as breath.

This applies to Christians too. Christianity is not the equivalent of a Get-out-of-Jail-Free card, granting us a lifelong exemption from either the least or the worst pain the world has to offer. While Jesus promises us he will be there to lead us through the valleys, he never promises that we will not enter them.

The question thus becomes how you handle the bad times. You can buckle to your knees in despair and cry, "Why me?" Or you can hit your knees in prayer and ask, "What do I do with this?"

Setbacks and tragedies are opportunities to reveal and to develop true character and abiding faith. Your faithfulness — not your skipping merrily along through life without pain — is what reveals the depth of your love for God.

It was a tough two weeks. I kept grinding.

— *Gerald Holmes*

**Faithfulness to God requires faith
even in — especially in — the bad times.**

IN A WORD

Read Matthew 12:33-37.

*"For out of the overflow of the heart the mouth speaks.
The good man brings good things out of the good stored
up in him, and the evil man brings evil things out of the
evil stored up in him" (vv. 34b-35).*

Magic Johnson was headed to Michigan — until a coach who wasn't even on the MSU staff anymore sat down with him and had a heart-to-heart talk.

Not surprisingly, the recruiting battle for one of the greatest players in basketball history was fierce. First-year head coach Jud Heathcote determined that the best way to recruit Johnson was to stay out of the way and let his coaching and the program's new direction do the talking.

As the winter of 1977 unwound, Michigan was pushing Johnson hard. The Spartans caught a break when Jay Vincent, Lansing's other high-school superstar that year, announced in March that he was signing with State. Vincent and Johnson were close enough to talk publicly about playing together in college.

Assistant coach Vern Payne wound up with the tricky part of Johnson's recruiting: the delicate contact work. He made sure he was seen and nothing more. State received a real setback, however, when Payne took the head coach's job at Wayne State.

Forty-eight hours before Johnson's announcement on April 22, Payne ran across two Michigan coaches at a local restaurant. He

SPARTANS

left convinced the Wolverines had Johnson in the bag.

Alarmed, Payne arranged to see Johnson at school and offered his final arguments for why he should choose Michigan State: He had always chosen the underdog and won; his potential at State transcended athletics; it was a matter of his roots and his heritage; he would elevate the standing of an entire community and city.

After listening to Payne's words, Johnson nodded and said, "I'll sign, Coach."

These days, everybody has something to say and likely as not a place to say it. Talk radio, 24-7 sports and news TV channels, late night talk shows. Texts. E-mails. If the price of something is measured by its abundance, then talk is cheap.

But words still have power, and that includes not just those of the talking heads, hucksters, and pundits on television, but ours also. Our words are perhaps the most powerful force we possess for good or for bad. The words we speak today can belittle, wound, humiliate, and destroy. They can also inspire, heal, protect, and create. Our words both shape and define us. They also reveal to the world the depth of our faith.

We should never make the mistake of underestimating the power of the spoken word. After all, speaking the Word was the only means Jesus had to get his message across — and look what he managed to do.

We must always watch what we say, because others sure will.

Next fall, I will be attending Michigan State University.
        — Magic Johnson's simple announcement of his decision

Choose your words carefully; they are the most powerful force you have for good or for bad.

DAZED & CONFUSED

Read Genesis 11:1-9.

"There the Lord confused the language of the whole world" (v. 9a).

Football buffs have called it "one of the classic upsets in the history" of college football. The game's ending was so confusing, however, that it took almost an hour to find out who won.

On Nov. 9, 1974, a heavily favored Ohio State team waltzed into Spartan Stadium. Featuring two-time Heisman Trophy winner Archie Griffin, the Buckeyes were undefeated and ranked No. 1; the Spartans of second-year coach Denny Stolz were 4-3-1.

With less than ten minutes left to play, the Buckeyes led 13-3 when Spartan quarterback Charlie Baggett tossed a strike to wide receiver Mike Jones for a 44-yard touchdown. The two-point conversion try failed, but MSU trailed only 13-9.

After a Buckeye punt, State was backed up to its 12-yard line. On the first play, fullback Levi Jackson broke through the right side of the line and sprinted down the sideline 88 yards for a touchdown. The venerable stadium came apart as MSU led 16-13.

Racing against time, Ohio State moved to the Spartan 1. Then with the clock ticking down to zero, the Buckeyes ran a play that ended up in the end zone. That's when confusion took over.

The referee signalled that the game had ended before the ball had been snapped. Another official signalled a touchdown. Fans stormed the field while players from both teams jumped up and down in celebration of a win. Up in the press box, no one was sure who had won the game. Big Ten commissioner Wayne Duke said he would find the officials and clear up the confusion.

That took a while because the refs had left the stadium. Finally, some 45 minutes after the game had ended, the public address announcer let everyone know that the 16-13 score was the official one. That ended the confusion but not the controversy.

Though it sometimes doesn't seem that way, confusion is not the natural order of things. God's universe — from the brilliant arrangement of DNA to the complex harmony of a millipede's legs to the dazzling array of the stars — is ordered. God's act of creation was at its most basic the bringing of order out of chaos.

So why then is confusion so pervasive in our society today? Why do so many of us struggle to make sense of our lives, foundering in our confusion over everything from our morals and values to our sexual orientation and our sense of what is right and what is wrong? The lesson of the Tower of Babel is instructive. That which God does not ordain he does not sustain. Thus, confusion is not the problem itself but is rather a symptom of the absence of God's will and God's power in our lives.

Confusion for the children of God is basically a sense of purposelessness. It fills the void in our lives that is created by a lack of intimacy with God.

Thirty seconds felt like a lifetime, the next hour like an eternity in purgatory.
— Writer Chris Solari on resolving the confusion at the '74 OSU game

In our lives, keeping confusion away
requires keeping God near.

COMEBACK KID

Read Luke 23:26-43.

"Then he said, 'Jesus remember me when you come into your kingdom.' Jesus answered him, 'I tell you the truth, today you will be with me in paradise'" (vv. 42-43).

Amp Campbell made a comeback that had pretty much been determined to be impossible.

A senior cornerback in 1998 headed for an NFL career, Campbell moved in for a touchdown-saving tackle against Oregon in the second game of the season. But he slipped and ducked his head, which slammed into the runner's thigh. It "kind of snapped my neck back a little bit," Campbell recalled.

It did much more than that. A burning sensation ran through his whole body. When he made it to the bench, he couldn't sit upright and his vision was blurred. At a hospital, X-rays revealed the worst: Campbell had fractured two vertebrae. He underwent spinal-fusion surgery that included drilling two holes in his skull for a halo to keep his head in place.

Six days after the surgery, Campbell walked into the Spartans' locker room prior to the Notre Dame game. During a team prayer, he broke down and cried. "If you have any pride, you'll win this one for Amp," declared tailback Sedrick Irvin. The Spartans did, clobbering the Irish 45-23.

As writer Adam Biggers put it, "The chances of coming back from a severe spinal cord injury like Campbell's are slim to none."

But Campbell "made the choice to do the unthinkable — return to finish his senior season."

Spartan head coach Nick Saban lent his support by lobbying the NCAA to allow Campbell a sixth year of eligibility. He made his unlikely return in the 1999 season opener during which he scooped up a fumble and returned it 85 yards for the game-winning touchdown — against Oregon.

But Campbell's incredible comeback was much more than that fairy-tale Oregon game. He went on to earn All-Big Ten honors.

Life will have its setbacks whether they result from personal failures or from forces and people beyond your control. Being a Christian and a faithful follower of Jesus Christ doesn't insulate you from getting into deep trouble. Maybe financial problems suffocated you or a serious illness or injury put you on the sidelines. Or your family was hit with a great tragedy.

Life is a series of victories and defeats. Winning isn't about avoiding defeat; it's about getting back up to compete again. It's about making a comeback of your own.

When you avail yourself of God's grace and God's power, your comeback is always greater than your setback. You are never too far behind, and it's never too late in life's game for Jesus to lead you to victory, to turn trouble into triumph. As it was with Amp Campbell and the penitent criminal crucified with Jesus, it's not how you start that counts; it's how you finish.

It is an amazing comeback story.
— *Mark Dantonio on Amp Campbell*

**No matter the circumstances in your life,
you can begin a comeback by turning to Jesus.**

MICHIGAN STATE

DAY 6

EASY DOES IT

Read John 6:53-66.

"[M]any of his disciples said, 'This is a hard teaching. Who can accept it?' . . . From this time many of his disciples turned back and no longer followed him" (vv. 60, 66).

The Spartans walked off the field in State College as Big Ten champions, but it wasn't easy.

Writer Jeremy Warnemuende declared that almost nobody saw the 2010 league title coming in the wake of a mediocre 6-7 season in 2009. Yet, here they were on Nov. 27, needing only a win over Penn State in Happy Valley to lay claim to an 11-win season, a top-10 ranking, and the title of Big Ten Champions.

Getting to that position hadn't been easy. State had fallen behind early against Purdue and Northwestern before rallying to win 35-31 and 35-27 respectively. The Spartans had survived an upset loss to Iowa and three first-half turnovers against 4th-ranked Wisconsin before winning 34-24. They had even managed to forge ahead when head coach Mark Dantonio suffered a heart attack following the win over Notre Dame. (See Devotion No. 42.)

"Our goal was to win the championship. That's our No. 1 goal," Dantonio had declared. And suddenly on a chilly night in Happy Valley, it all seemed so easy. The Spartans scored on their opening drive with Edwin Baker getting the touchdown on a 7-yard run to the pylon. For three quarters, MSU was never headed, roaring to

SPARTANS

an 18-point lead heading into the final fifteen minutes.

And then it wasn't easy anymore. Penn State suddenly put it together after bumbling around all night. The Nittany Lions scored 19 points to close to 28-22 with 56 ticks on the clock. Only when the Spartans recovered the onsides kick could they rest easy.

"We could've ended it easily at 28-10, but we'll take it," Dantonio said in his post-game interview.

Beating a quality opponent such as Penn State or Michigan is never easy, no matter what the sport. Neither is following Jesus.

It's not just the often abstruse aspects of Jesus' teachings that test us mentally. It's that Jesus demands disruption in our lives. To take even a hesitant, tentative step toward following Jesus is to take a gigantic stride toward changing our lives — and change is never easy. In fact, we abhor it; all too often we choose to live in misery and unhappiness because it's familiar. Something about the devil we know being safer than the angel we don't.

Jesus also demands commitment. We who live in a secular, me-first age are to surrender our lives to him. We are to think, act, live, and feel in a way totally counter to the prevailing philosophy of the world we temporarily call home. We are to keep our sights on the spiritual world and spend our lives in service and sacrifice now in exchange for a future eternal reward.

None of that is easy. But neither was dying on a cross.

We can't do it the easy way, can we?
— Quarterback Kirk Cousins after the Penn State win

That which is easily accomplished in life
is rarely satisfying or rewarding;
this includes our following Jesus.

UNSTOPPABLE!

Read Acts 5:29-42.

"If it is from God, you will not be able to stop these men; you will only find yourselves fighting against God" (v. 39).

L.J. Scott was unstoppable, and, thus, so was Michigan State's march to the championship of the Big Ten.

On Dec. 5, 2015, the 5th-ranked Spartans and the undefeated, 4th-ranked Iowa Hawkeyes met in the Big Ten Championship Game. Almost 67,000 fans were treated to a glimpse into the past, to a time when defenses dominated, play was physical, and offenses struggled for yardage and points. Yards were so precious that the game ultimately came down to just one of them.

After an 85-yard touchdown pass on the first play of the fourth quarter, Iowa led 13-9. With its title and playoff hopes on the verge of slipping away, State answered with an epic drive. It consumed nine minutes and four seconds, required 22 plays, and covered 82 yards. "The season on the line, [quarterback Connor] Cook and the offense made play after play against an Iowa defense that hadn't give up a touchdown all night."

Nothing came easy on the drive. With 1:59 to play, State faced a fourth-and-2 at the Iowa 5. Cook got the two yards on a keeper that was so close it required a measurement.

After that, Scott, a freshman running back, had the game and the ball put in his hands. He carried to the 1 and then was hit for no gain. On third down, as Scott put it, "I was just trying to make a big play for my brothers." He did and became part of MSU lore.

He ran into a wall at the 1, but he would not be stopped even as the Iowa defenders ganged up on him and pushed him backward. On a play that eventually took six interminable seconds, Scott stayed on his feet, lunged forward, stretched, and reached the ball into the end zone with 27 seconds left. The extra point wrapped up a 16-13 win and the championship.

When his team needed him most, L.J. Scott was unstoppable.

Isn't that the way we would like our lives to unfold? Lodging one success after another in our careers, our families, our investments, whatever it is we try? Unstoppable. The reality, however, is that life isn't like that at all. At some point, we all run into setbacks that stop us dead in our tracks. Everyone does — except God.

For almost two thousand years, the enemies of God have tried to stop Jesus and his people. They killed Jesus; they have persecuted and martyred his followers. Today, heretics and infidels — many of them in America — are more active in their war on Christianity than at any other time in history.

And yet, the Kingdom of God advances, unstoppable despite all opposition. Pursuing God's purposes in our lives puts us on a team bound for glory. Fighting against God gets his enemies nowhere. Except Hell.

A half-dozen Iowa defenders tried to stop [L.J.] Scott and pushed him backward, but he wouldn't be denied.
— BigTen.org on L.J. Scott's unstoppable touchdown run vs. Iowa

**God's kingdom and purposes are unstoppable
no matter what his enemies try.**

LIKE CLOCKWORK

Read Matthew 25:1-13.

"Keep watch, because you do not know the day or the hour" (v. 13).

The 2001 Michigan game will forever remain one of the most controversial games in series history — because of the clock.

The mere mention of "Clockgate" to any Wolverine or Spartan fan with a sense of the history of the series will elicit a reaction ranging from a knowing chuckle to wounded outrage. On Nov. 3, the Wolverines showed up at Spartan Stadium ranked No. 6 in the nation while State was 4-2.

The Wolverines led 24-20. With only 2:28 left to play, a 28-yard Michigan punt gave the Spartans one final shot from the U-M 44. On fourth-and-4 at the Michigan 11, sophomore quarterback Jeff Smoker completed a pass to running back T.J. Duckett, who rushed for 211 yards that day, down to the 3. The Spartans were out of timeouts, so Smoker hurriedly spiked the ball with 17 seconds to play.

On second down, Smoker was flushed out of the pocket and ran to the 2 but was tackled inbounds. He managed to line his team up and spike the ball, but how much time was left? The clock said one second. Michigan's coaches and the *ABC* broadcasters argued that clock operator Bob Stehlin, known widely as "Spartan Bob," had stopped the clock before the play was over.

Smoker, whose total of 3,395 passing yards in 2003 remains the

SPARTANS

school single-season record, used that one second to loft a pass to Duckett for a touchdown and a stunning 26-24 win.

Controversy about that one second erupted immediately. The Wolverine radio announcer called the incident "criminal." Stehlin received threatening calls and letters, including one from a Wolverine fan advising him to pray for forgiveness.

Big Ten officials reviewed the play and determined that "Spartan Bob" had acted appropriately. "Clockgate" did, however, lead to the use of an official timekeeper appointed by the league.

We may pride ourselves on our time management, but the truth is that we don't manage time; it manages us. Hurried and harried, we live by schedules that seem to have too much what and too little when. By setting the bedside alarm at night, we even let the clock determine how much down time we get. A life of leisure actually means one in which time is of no importance.

Every second of our life — all the time we have — is a gift from God, who came up with the notion of time in the first place. We would do well, therefore, to consider what God considers to be good time management. After all, Jesus warned us against mismanaging the time we have. From God's point of view, using our time wisely means being prepared at every moment for Jesus' return, which will occur — well, only time will tell when.

That play, as much as we've put [it] under a high-powered microscope, was correct. We could not prove that timer wrong.
— Big Ten Coordinator of Officials Dave Parry on 'Clockgate'

**We mismanage our time when we fail
to prepare for Jesus' return even though
we don't know when that will be.**

DAY 9

BLOOD TYPE

Read Hebrews 9:12-28.

"[W]ithout the shedding of blood there is no forgiveness"
(v. 22b).

Micajah Reynolds had clothes drenched in blood to remind him of the night he helped save a teenager's life.

From 2010-13, Reynolds was a four-year letterwinner for the Spartans. He saw action on both sides of the line, primarily as a defensive tackle. For his play in the 24-20 win over Stanford in the 2014 Rose Bowl, *ESPN* named him to the Big Ten All-Bowl team.

On July 31 before his senior season, Reynolds was heading home after visiting a friend. The hour was late, traffic was light, and the streets were empty. Suddenly, though, his peaceful drive was interrupted when he spotted someone trying to flag him down. A second look revealed the man was bleeding.

Reynolds pulled a U-turn in the middle of the street, jumped out of his car, and ran over to the man. "He had been shot in the head," Reynolds said. So the Spartan set about doing what he could to help what turned out to be an 18-year-old robbery victim who had been shot multiple times.

Reynolds used his shirt and applied pressure to the wounds to staunch the bleeding. He also comforted the teen, telling him he was going to be all right. "I felt like I was spotting someone on the bench and being like, 'Man, you can do it,'" he said. "'Just relax and keep going. You got it.'"

Thanks in large part to Reynolds' aid, the teen pulled through. The incident left the Spartan senior with some bloody clothes and some serious reflections. "Life is so delicate," he said. Something like that "makes you consider and be thankful and so grateful for everything that you're given."

The Christian lexicon makes much to-do about "blood." Its context, however, is always related to the bloody death of Christ on the cross.

In the Old Testament, somewhat to our horror and our dismay, we find a sacrificial system in which the killing of an animal is required to reconcile man and God. The creator of all life dictated that life be taken to save us from the separation from God resulting from our sins. This dramatically and shockingly underscores just how seriously God takes sin, even if we don't.

The death of Christ on the cross marked the beginning of the New Covenant and the culmination of the sacrificial system. In other words, Christ's death wasn't novel at all; it was in keeping with the sacrificial system established on Mt. Sinai.

But it was vastly different. This was God in the flesh that was slaughtered. He was the perfect sacrifice, rendering any other attempt at reconciliation ineffectual and futile. We don't have to kill and burn pigeons, doves, and heifers to get right with God. Instead, we have our faith in Jesus, who shed his blood for us.

I've still got my shirt and all my clothes over at the house that are completely drenched in his blood.
— Micajah Reynolds, after helping to save a teen's life

The blood of Jesus makes forgiveness possible;
faith in Jesus makes forgiveness certain.

DAY 10

NAME DROPPING

Read Exodus 3:13-20.

"God said to Moses, 'I AM WHO I AM. This is what you are to say to the Israelites: 'I AM has sent me to you''" (v. 14).

Michigan State landed a nickname because a sportswriter didn't like the one the school had and came up with his own.

In 1925, the school's name was changed from Michigan Agricultural College to Michigan State College. The old nickname of the "Aggies" was thus no longer appropriate, so the college sponsored a contest to select a new name. The rather unfortunate winner was "The Michigan Staters."

George S. Alderton, sports editor of the *Lansing State Journal*, determined that the name was too cumbersome for newspaper writing. Setting out to find a better one, he contacted Jim Hasselman of the college's information services to learn if any of the contest entries had not been discarded. Some had not, so he sifted through them. When he ran across the entry name of "Spartans," Alderton decided that was the one. He failed to write down who submitted the name, so that bit of history remains a mystery.

The new "Spartans" nickname made its first appearance in print in the spring of 1926 when the school baseball team went on a training tour in the South. Perry Fremont, a catcher, supplied Alderton with game accounts. The editor used the Spartan nickname sparingly in his first articles before making the leap and using it in a headline. Dale Stafford, a sportswriter for the *Lansing Capitol News*, picked up on the name for his paper. And so it has been the Spartans ever since.

(As an aside, Alderton spelled the name incorrectly with an "o" in his first accounts. A close friend informed him of the error.)

The "Spartans" notwithstanding, nicknames are not usually slapped haphazardly upon individuals but rather reflect widely held perceptions about the person named. Proper names can also have a particular physical or character trait associated with them.

Nowhere throughout the long march of history has this concept been more prevalent than in the Bible, where a name is not a mere label but is an expression of the essential nature of the named one. That is, a person's name reveals his or her character. This applies even to God; to know the name of God is to know God as he has chosen to reveal himself to us.

What does your name say about you? Honest, trustworthy, a seeker of the truth and a person of God? Or does the mention of your name cause your coworkers to whisper snide remarks, your neighbors to roll their eyes, or your friends to start making allowances for you?

Most importantly, what does your name say about you to God? He, too, knows you by name.

No [one] called up the editor to complain about our audacity in giving the old school a new name. Happily for the experiment, the name took.
— George S. Alderton on the birth of the 'Spartans' nickname

**Live so that your name evokes positive
associations by people you know,
by the public, and by God.**

BIG DEAL

Read Ephesians 3:1-13.

*"His intent was that now, through the church, the
manifold wisdom of God should be made known" (v. 10).*

It started as a throwaway idea at a party. It wound up as the biggest deal in the history of hockey to that point.

In January 2001, assistant hockey coach Dave McAuliffe rather laughingly and wildly suggested that a hockey game at Spartan Stadium would be "a nifty event." After all, hockey had been one of State's Big Three sports for decades, a consistent winner and a box-office smash with a deep and devoted fan base.

McAuliffe's suggestion was greeted with a round of grins at the sponsor's party at which he offered it up. Associate athletic director Mark Hollis grinned along with everyone else, but he didn't let it go and began checking with companies that installed ice surfaces. The idea grew until head coach Ron Mason, athletic director Clarence Underwood, and associate AD Greg Ianni made a formal presentation to the school's president and vice-president.

They bought it.

Tickets went on sale in June for a game on Oct. 6 against Michigan. It was dubbed The Cold War. Concerns that such an oddity wouldn't click with the fan base were soon alleviated. Hours after the ducats went on sale, the line at the ticket office was out the door. The event would go on to be a sell-out: 74,554, the largest crowd ever to watch a hockey game.

Worries about the weather deepened when a temporary rink was set up early in the week. Amid unseasonably warm temperatures, it melted and flooded. Only seventy-two hours before face-off, waves splashed against the boards.

"Let's not do it," Mason said, convinced a disaster was in the making. But cooler air arrived in time, and the game went on. Freshman Jim Slater tied it for the Spartans with 47 seconds left in regulation. Neither team scored in the overtime.

The unfolding of our lives is marked by big deals even if they aren't outdoor hockey games. Our wedding, childbirth, a new job, a new house, big MSU games, even a new car. What we regard as a big deal is what shapes not only our lives but our character.

One of the most unfathomable anomalies of faith in America today is that while many people profess to be die-hard Christians, they disdain involvement with a local church. As Paul tells us, however, the Church is a very big deal to God; it is at the heart of his redemptive work; it is a vital part of his eternal purposes.

The Church is no accident of history. It isn't true that Jesus died and all he wound up with for his troubles was the stinking Church. It is no consolation prize.

Rather, the Church is the primary instrument through which God's plan of cosmic and eternal salvation is worked out. And it doesn't get any bigger than that.

Pulling off an outdoor hockey game in a football stadium [was] a Hollywood-grade production.
— Sportswriter Lynn Henning on the big deal that was The Cold War

To disdain church involvement is to assert that God doesn't know what he's doing.

MYSTERIOUS WAYS

Read Romans 11:25-36.

"O the depth of the riches and wisdom and knowledge of God! How unsearchable are his judgments and how inscrutable his ways!" (v. 33 NRSV)

There's no mystery about "MSU Shadows" being the school's alma mater. For some time, however, the same could not be said about the song's composer.

In 1907, Michigan Agricultural College adopted "Close Beside the Winding Cedar" as its alma mater. The music was taken from Cornell's alma mater. In the 1940s, the students at Michigan State College wanted a song of their own, so they voted and chose "MSU Shadows." In March 1949, the song was officially ratified as the school's alma mater.

Mystery and controversy swirled about the song's composer. The widespread understanding was that it had been written in 1927 by Bernard Traynor, who was the college's football line coach from 1925-27. He also served as coach of the freshman basketball team. Traynor wrote the melody and the lyrics; Leonard Falcone, MSU's director of bands from 1927-67, provided the arrangement that is played today by the Spartan Marching Band.

But as MSU gained national exposure in the 1950s, so did its fight song and alma mater, and copyright issues arose. "A slew of correspondence" between MSU and various record companies went back and forth. One claim frequently made and discounted was that the melody was "borrowed" from an opera.

A "dubious claim from out of the blue" asserted that somebody named Lucille Morris was a co-composer. It was eventually determined she was a figment of someone's vivid imagination.

The furor gradually subsided as the mystery was decided in favor of Coach Traynor.

People of faith understand, as the old saying goes, that the good Lord works in mysterious ways. This serves to make God even more tantalizing because human nature loves a good mystery. We relish the challenge of uncovering what somebody else wants to hide. We are intrigued by a perplexing whodunit such as *NCIS*, a rousing round of Clue, or *Perry Mason* and *Matlock* reruns.

Unlike the controversy about "MSU Shadows," some mysteries are simply beyond our knowing, however. Events in our lives that are in actuality the mysterious ways of God remain so to us because we can't see the divine machinations. We can see only the results, appreciate that God was behind it all, and give him thanks and praise.

God has revealed much about himself, especially through Jesus, but still much remains unknowable. Why does he tolerate the existence of evil? What does he really look like? Why is he so fond of bugs? What was the inspiration for chocolate?

We know for sure, though, that God is love, and so we proceed with life, assured that one day all mysteries will be revealed.

All kinds of claims and counterclaims were thrown around.
— Writer Robert Bao on the 'mystery' surrounding 'MSU Shadows'

God keeps much about himself shrouded in
mystery, but one day we will see and understand.

DAY 13

DANCING MACHINE

Read 2 Samuel 6:12-22.

"David danced before the Lord with all his might, while he and the entire house of Israel brought up the ark of the Lord with shouts and the sound of trumpets" (vv. 14-15).

The Spartans' defeat of Wisconsin was so sudden and exciting that it left Mark Dantonio dancing.

On Oct. 27, 2012, State trotted into Camp Randall Stadium a decided underdog. The Badgers were ranked 25th and had won 21 straight home games, second-longest streak in the country.

Both defenses dominated. *ESPN's* Adam Rittenberg termed Spartan defensive end William Gholston "an absolute beast" with 4.5 tackles for loss. Linebacker Max Bullough led the team with nine tackles with 2.5 tackles for loss. For the game, the defense held Wisconsin "to an astounding" 19 rushing yards on 37 tries.

The Wisconsin defense likewise dominated the Spartan offense until it seemed as though the "Badgers would escape with an ugly [10-3] win." On its first five possessions of the last half, the MSU offense managed one first down, one fumble, and zero points.

But then State came alive and put together a 12-play, 75-yard drive as the clock ran down in the fourth quarter. Quarterback Andrew Maxwell completed 8 of 9 passes on the drive. The last one was a 4-yard touchdown pass to Big-Ten rushing leader Le'-Veon Bell with 1:08 left that tied the game at 10.

Wisconsin managed a field goal on its possession in overtime.

SPARTANS

The game ended suddenly and dramatically when Maxwell hit "a seemingly blanketed Bennie Fowler" with a 12-yard TD pass.

With a demeanor often described as dour and buttoned down, Dantonio got caught up in the excitement in the postgame locker room. He let loose with a "dance" that was caught on video. The Spartan boss described his moves as "just an up-and-down deal"; chants of "Hey!" by the players accompanied his boogie moves.

One of the more enduring stereotypes of the Christian is of an unhappy, sour-faced person always on the prowl to sniff out fun and frivolity and shut it down. "Somewhere, sometime, somebody's having fun — and it's got to stop!" Many understand this to be the mandate that governs the Christian life.

But nothing could be further from reality or the truth. Ages ago King David, he who would eventually number Jesus Christ among his house and lineage, set the standard for those who love and worship the Lord when he danced in the presence of God with unrestrained joy. Many centuries and one savior later, David's example today reminds us that a life spent in an awareness of God's presence is all about celebrating, rejoicing, and enjoying God's countless gifts, including salvation in Jesus Christ.

Yes, dancing can be vulgar and coarse, but as with David, God looks into our hearts to see what is there. Our very life should be one long song and dance for Jesus.

Everybody was just doing their deal. Can't beat' em, join 'em, so . . . ."
— Mark Dantonio on his post-Wisconsin dance

While dancing and music can be vulgar and obscene, they can also be inspiring expressions of abiding love for God.

GREAT EXPECTATIONS

Read John 1:43-51.

"'Nazareth! Can anything good come from there?'
Nathanael asked" (v. 46).

Expectations were so low for the 1955 Spartans that even the school's sports information office declared the club "isn't likely to produce a big winning season." So much for that.

Duffy Daugherty retired in 1972 after 19 season as State's head football coach. He won 109 games and two national titles and was inducted into the College Football Hall of Fame in 1984.

After a 3-6 record in 1954, Daugherty's first season, "not much was expected of the 1955 season despite Duffy's chronic optimism." The team turned those tepid expectations upside down, however, by winning nine games, including the Rose Bowl.

The first step toward a great season occurred after one week of fall practice. That's how long it took Daugherty to name Earl Morrall the starting quarterback. He had an All-American season.

The season opened with a 20-13 defeat of Indiana. That unimpressive win over a bad Hoosier team and a 14-7 loss to Michigan the following week did little to change the tempered expectations. Two weeks later, however, the Spartans whipped a good Notre Dame squad 21-7. The team did not have another close game all season and "hurtled [its] way to glory."

The final game of the season was a 33-0 wasting of Marquette. Sixty-five miles away, Michigan was hosting Ohio State; if the

SPARTANS

Buckeyes won, the Spartans would head to the Rose Bowl.

The athletic department waived its rule against radios in the stands that day, and the result was "a series of fantastic, funny crowd reactions." One time fans broke into a mighty cheer as a 15-yard penalty was being walked off against State. Even the State players on the sidelines huddled up against the nearest radio.

Ohio State won, and the team of which little was expected finished the season 8-1 and then beat UCLA in the Rose Bowl.

The blind date your friend promised would look just like Ryan Reynolds or Jennifer Lawrence but instead resembled Cousin Itt or an extra in a zombie flick. Your vacation of a lifetime that went downhill after the lost luggage. Often your expectations are raised only to be dashed.

Perhaps most devastating of all to your self-esteem, however, is when you realize that you are the one not meeting the expectations other people have for you. The truth is, though, that you aren't here to live up to what others think of you. Jesus didn't; in part, that's why they killed him. But he did meet God's expectations for his life, which was all that really mattered.

Because God's kingdom is so great, God does have great expectations for any who would enter, and you should not take them lightly. What the world expects from you is of no importance; what God expects from you is paramount.

State appears to be at least a year away from having a top-flight outfit.
— 1955 preseason sheet from the sports information office

You have little if anything to gain from meeting the world's expectations of you; you have all of eternity to gain from meeting God's.

MAKE NO MISTAKES

Read Mark 14:66-72.

"Then Peter remembered the word Jesus had spoken to him: 'Before the rooster crows twice you will disown me three times.' And he broke down and wept" (v. 72).

Two mistakes once occurred in the Spartan locker room at half-time of a basketball game: one by the head coach and one by a player who called him on it.

The last game the national champions of 1979 would lose came in the regular season finale against Wisconsin, an 83-81 defeat. Head coach Jud Heathcote wasn't too happy at halftime. In fact, he was described as "ranting and raving" in the locker room.

He was particularly distressed by what he perceived to be Wisconsin's rebounding edge. "We're getting killed on the boards," Heathcote hollered at his silent players. "We must be down by 10 rebounds or more. Can't anybody get a rebound?"

About that time, a student manager walked up and handed the coach the game's stat sheet. Heathcote looked at it for a moment in dismay before shaking his head. "It says here we're one rebound up," he said in obvious disbelief. "There must be a mistake."

For a moment, the room endured an awkward silence. Then came a voice from the back, that of Greg "Boobie" Lloyd, a reserve guard often described as "free spirited." He appeared in nineteen games that season, scoring 27 points. Lloyd had only three words to say, but they were shockers: "Stats . . . don't . . . lie."

Heathcote looked up from the stat sheet, glared at Lloyd, and then said to assistant coach Bill Berry, "Get him out of here." "It's awfully funny now, but nobody could believe he said it at that time," recalled forward Don Brkovich. "Nobody reacted . . . except for Gregory Kelser, who had a little smirk on his face."

The Badgers did wind up outrebounding State though Kelser pulled down ten caroms, enough to make him State's all-time career rebounding leader. (Draymond Green has the record now.)

It's distressing but it's true: We all make mistakes. Only one perfect man ever walked on this earth, and no one of us is he. Some mistakes are just dumb. Like locking yourself out of your home or walking facefirst into a sliding glass door.

Other mistakes are more significant and carry with them the potential for devastation. Like heading down a path to addiction. Committing a crime. Walking out on a spouse and the children.

All these mistakes, however, from the momentarily annoying to the life-altering tragic, share one aspect: They can all be forgiven in Christ. Other folks may not forgive us; we may not even forgive ourselves. But God will forgive us when we call upon him in Jesus' name.

Thus, the twofold fatal mistake we can make is ignoring the fact that we will die one day and subsequently ignoring the fact that Jesus is the only way to shun Hell and enter Heaven. We absolutely must get this one right.

I was kind of a free spirit and was always getting in Jud's doghouse.
— Greg Lloyd on calling coach Jud Heathcote out

Only one mistake we make sends us to Hell when we die: ignoring Jesus while we live.

WE JUST DISAGREE

Read Romans 14:13-23.

"For the kingdom of God is not a matter of eating and drinking, but of righteousness, peace and joy in the Holy Spirit" (v. 17).

George Webster and Charlie Thornhill were arguing at such lengths that the opposing team's halfback told them to shut up.

The two were stalwarts of State's legendary defenses of 1965 and '66, which finished number two in the nation in total defense both seasons. The Spartans were national champions both years.

As a senior linebacker, Thornhill led the team in tackles in 1966 and earned first-team All-Big Ten honors. Webster was the star of the defense, a player so versatile no one was really sure what position he played. Head coach Duffy Daugherty ultimately created a new position for him: monster man. He told Webster to line up where he thought it was best to be, to play the whole field.

Turned loose, Webster became a Spartan legend. He was a two-time All-America, and his number 90 was the second to be retired by the university. He was elected to the College Football Hall of Fame in 1987. In 1999, *Sports Illustrated* named him one of the starting safeties on its all-century team.

Webster and Thornhill shared a unique chemistry on the field. "George would say, 'Which way is [the play] going, Dog?'" Thornhill recalled. "And I'd say, 'To the right.'" They would then compete to see who could make the tackle first.

SPARTANS

That competitiveness and chemistry showed up in the 1966 opener against North Carolina State (a 28-10 win). They reached the State halfback at the same time and dropped him for a loss. They then started arguing about who had made the tackle. Finally, the frustrated State back yelled at them to "cut it out so he could get up and get back to the huddle."

The only time folks haven't disagreed among themselves was when Adam roamed the garden alone. Since then — well, we just can't seem to get along.

That includes Christians, who have never exactly been role models for peaceful coexistence among themselves. Not only does the greater body of Christ always seem to be spatting and feuding, but discord within individual churches is so commonplace that God uses church splits to grow his kingdom.

Why can't Christians get along? Perhaps it's because we take our faith so seriously, which is a good thing. But perhaps also, it's because — as Paul warned — we sometimes fail to discern the difference between what is important and what is trivial.

Following Christ is about achieving righteousness, joy, and peace, not about following arcane, arbitrary prescriptions for daily living or even worship. All too often we don't get along because the rules and traditions we espouse — and not Christ's love — govern our hearts and our faith.

Between the two of us, we'd have a play read, and then we'd just see who could get there for the tackle first.
— Charlie Thornhill on the chemistry between George Webster and him

Christians will never get along as long as we worry about and harp on things that we shouldn't.

DAY 17

REVELATION

Read Isaiah 53.

*"But he was pierced for our transgressions, he was
crushed for our iniquities; the punishment that brought us
peace was upon him, and by his wounds we are healed"
(v. 5).*

Sedrick Irvin made such a ridiculous prophecy that virtually
no one paid any attention to him. They should have.

As the clock ticked down on the Ohio State game of Nov. 7, 1998,
Irvin, a junior tailback, turned to a group of reporters standing
behind the end line and shouted, "I told you! I told you! I told you
we were gonna shock the world!"

He had told them, and what the Spartans pulled off that day
did indeed send shock waves across college football. MSU was
only 4-4 for the season while the Buckeyes had pretty much been
conceded one of the slots in the BCS championship game. So little
was expected of the Spartans that Ohio State entered the game
a 27.5-point favorite. Nevertheless, Irvin boldly predicted a State
win to anyone who would listen.

For much of the game, Irvin's prediction looked as foolhardy
as most folks thought it was. Ohio State led 24-9 with 9:51 to go
in the third quarter. But the Spartans rallied behind Bill Burke's
touchdown toss to Lavaile Richardson, a field goal from Paul
Edinger, and a 92-yard drive capped off by Irvin's 3-yard run.

With 14:20 to play, MSU led 25-24; "the OSU fans were stunned, and their heroes were shaken." "That's when it really started creeping into our minds: 'Hey, this can actually happen,'" said freshman guard Paul Harker. "They were starting to get intimidated."

It took a late defensive stand to make it happen, but Irvin's fantastical prophecy came true with a 28-24 win. "If you see Lee Corso or Kirk Herbstreit of *ESPN*, or anyone else who said we'd be lucky to lose 41-10, give them my beeper number," Irvin said.

In our jaded age, we have pretty much relegated prophecy to dark rooms in which mysterious women peer into crystal balls or clasp our sweaty palms while uttering some vague generalities. At best, we understand a prophet as someone who predicts future events such as the outcome of football games as Sedrick Irvin did.

Within the pages of the Bible, though, we encounter something radically different. A prophet is a messenger from God, one who relays divine revelation to others.

Prophets seem somewhat foreign to us because in one very real sense the age of prophecy is over. In the name of Jesus, we have access to God through our prayers and through scripture. In searching for God's will for our lives, we seek divine revelation. We may speak only for ourselves and not for the greater body of Christ, but we do not need a prophet to discern what God would have us do. We need faith in the one whose birth, life, and death fulfilled more than 300 Bible prophecies.

For one wondrous evening in Columbus, Ohio, Sedrick Irvin was a very satisfied football prophet.
— *Sportswriter Joe Rexrode*

**Persons of faith continuously seek
a word from God for their lives.**

GOD'S CONQUERORS

Read John 16:19-33.

"In this world you will have trouble. But take heart! I have overcome the world" (v. 33b).

From the time when he pulled a pot of boiling spaghetti off a stove, Kirk Cousin's life has been about overcoming the odds.

Cousins finished his career in East Lansing in 2011 as the greatest quarterback in school history to that time. Among others, he set records for wins, passing yards, and touchdown passes. (Records subsequently broken by Connor Cook (2012-16).) In 2011, he won the Lowe's Senior CLASS Award, presented to the most outstanding student-athlete in NCAA's Division I FBS.

None of it — indeed, not much of anything in Cousins' life — came easy. His battle against the odds began when he was 19 months old and had that awful encounter with the boiling pasta. When his clothes were removed from his upper torso, a layer of skin came with them. He spent two weeks in the hospital and had to wear a jacket to compress the skin for almost a year. "It was horrific for all of us," said his father, Don, a pastor. Doctors said he would heal but would never be able to throw a ball properly.

In the sixth grade, Cousins played tackle football for the first time. The coach relegated him to the B-team. All he did was lead the team to the league championship. As a sophomore, he was told he wasn't good enough to play on the varsity baseball team. He chose to stay anyhow and became the starting third baseman.

SPARTANS

He started his junior season as the basketball team's third-string point guard. He moved into the starting lineup his first game.

When Cousins played his last high school football game, he didn't have a major scholarship offer. He landed a scholarship only after more highly recruited quarterbacks turned State down. Even then, he wasn't expected to play.

"The fact is he's been overlooked and underestimated most of his life," said the senior Cousins about his son's obstacles.

And each step along the way, Kirk Cousins has overcome.

We often hear inspiring stories of people who triumph by overcoming especially daunting obstacles. Those barriers may be physical or mental disabilities or great personal tragedies or injustice. When we hear of them, we may well respond with a little prayer of thanksgiving that life has been kinder to us.

But all people of faith, no matter how drastic the obstacles they face, must ultimately overcome the same opponent: the Satan-infested world. Some do have it tougher than others, but we all must fight daily to remain confident and optimistic.

To merely survive from day to day is to give up by surrendering our trust in God's involvement in our daily life. To overcome, however, is to stand up to the world and fight its temptations that would erode the armor of our faith in Jesus Christ.

Today is a day for you to overcome by remaining faithful. The very hosts of Heaven wait to hail the conquering hero.

My life has been living evidence of God's ability to do the unexplainable.
— Kirk Cousins on overcoming the odds

**Life's difficulties provide us a chance to
experience the true joy of victory in Jesus.**

GOOD IDEA

Read Luke 8:40-56.

"In the presence of all the people, she told why she had touched him" (v. 47).

Head coach Tom Izzo came up with turned out to be a really good idea: Practice his basketball team in football pads.

As he watched a replay of the Ohio State game of Jan. 20, 2000, on the flight home from Columbus, Izzo was furious. The squad that had advanced to the Final Four the season before and had figured to make it there again had lost and fallen to 12-5. Most galling of all for Izzo was the way they had lost: They had been pushed around, displaying an appalling lack of toughness. Izzo determined that would change immediately.

When the players arrived for practice the next morning, their first hint that something was up came when they realized there were no basketballs in sight. They watched with growing uneasiness as equipment manager Dave Pruder rolled a cart onto the floor that was loaded with football equipment.

The players were told to suit up: helmets and shoulder pads. They were then positioned in "one-on-one gladiator standoffs [and] urged to belt away." For players like Mateen Cleaves and Andre Hutson, who had been football stars in high school, the exercise gave them a chance to rekindle an old passion. Other players were a little more intimidated. It didn't take long, though, before Breslin Center sounded like "a high-decibel popcorn machine [as] helmets and plastic slapped and clacked." Players got "into the spirit of coaching-monitored mayhem."

Next came the War Drill, basically a basketball free-for-all. The presence of the pads amounted to an invitation to turn the drill into a blood bath. It delighted Izzo no end.

So did the results. When the pads came off, the team had its "best pure basketball practice of the season." Soft no more, they lost only twice more, finished 32-7, and won the national title.

Like Tom Izzo's brainchild that January morning, you've probably had a few moments of inspiration, divine or otherwise, yourself. Attending Michigan State or becoming a Spartan fan, marrying that person you did, maybe going back to school or starting a business or a family: they were good ideas.

From climbing aboard a horse's back to anesthesia to Double Stuf Oreos, good ideas are nothing new. The trouble is they're usually pretty hard to come by — except for the one that is right there before us all.

That woman with the bleeding problem had it. So did Jarius, the synagogue ruler. They had a big problem in their lives, so they came up with the notion that they should turn to Jesus and trust in him for help, hope, and deliverance.

It was a good idea then; it's a good idea now, the best ever, in fact. Surrendering your life to Jesus is such a good idea that its effects reverberate through all eternity.

Breslin Center was about to transform into Spartan Stadium.
— Writer Lynn Henning on Tom Izzo's idea to use football pads

Good ideas are hard to come by except for
the best idea of all: giving your life to Jesus.

DAY 20

TOUGH AS NAILS

Read 2 Corinthians 11:21b-29.

"Besides everything else, I face daily the pressure of my concern for all the churches" (v. 28).

When the three Allen brothers arrived in East Lansing to play football, they already know about being tough. They had learned it at home growing up.

Center Jack Allen was the first to arrive. He was First-Team All-America as a senior in 2015 and scored a touchdown against Penn State on a handoff. Brother Brian showed up in 2014 and was a Freshman All-America playing guard and center. He moved into the starting lineup as a sophomore. Matt the youngest, followed in brother Jack's footsteps as a center. He joined the squad in the fall of 2016 and was redshirted.

The trio gained part of the toughness required of a successful offensive lineman from an early introduction to wrestling. The boys' father wrestled at Purdue; an uncle, Jim Zajicek, wrestled and played football at Northwestern. They had the boys in singlets "shortly after they learned to tie their shoes." All three boys developed into college-caliber wrestlers, as tough as nails.

The family put a wrestling mat in the basement, which wound up costing a small fortune in drywall replacements. The brotherly bouts turned even more rambunctious when the boys got boxing gloves one Christmas. The mat thus became more of "an anything-goes fight zone." In fact, the boys grappled anywhere they could find a flat surface. Jack and Brian even wrestled in hotel rooms when they were on the road together with the State football team.

Brian has said the worst spot for him was the family trampoline with its tall netting and lone exit when he was in the second or third grade. His only means of escape was through Jack, who was older and stronger. Some of the fights, he said, he'd rather forget even if they did toughen him up some.

You don't have to be a Michigan State lineman like Jack, Brian, and Matt Allen to be tough. In America today, toughness isn't restricted to physical accomplishments and brute strength. Going to work every morning even when you feel bad, sticking by your rules for your children in a society that ridicules parental authority, making hard decisions about your aging parents' care often over their objections — you've got to be tough every day just to live honorably, decently, and justly.

Living faithfully requires toughness, too, though in America chances are you won't be imprisoned, stoned, or flogged this week for your faith as Paul was. Still, contemporary society exerts subtle, psychological, daily pressures on you to turn your back on your faith and your values. Popular culture promotes promiscuity, atheism, and gutter language; your children's schools have kicked God out; the corporate culture advocates amorality before the shrine of the almighty dollar.

You have to hang tough to keep the faith.

The Allen brothers set themselves apart with their toughness.
— MSU Co-offensive coordinator Jim Bollman

Life demands more than mere physical toughness;
you must be spiritually tough too.

NO APOLOGIES

Read Acts 4:1-21.

"For we cannot help speaking about what we have seen and heard" (v. 20).

The Drew Stanton era at Michigan State began when he apologized to his teammates at halftime.

Stanton was set to start in 2003 at quarterback as a redshirt freshman. But Jeff Smoker, who had been brilliant in 2001 before missing the 2002 season, was cleared to play. "He was a no-brainer over any redshirt freshman."

A severe knee injury in the bowl game meant Stanton was physically not ready to play as the 2004 season began. He was the third-string quarterback behind senior Damon Dowdell and redshirt freshman Stephen Reaves.

Dowdell got the nod, but when State lost the opener at Rutgers, head coach John L. Smith turned to Reaves. He played well in a win over Central Michigan but threw three interceptions in the first half against Notre Dame. Smith tapped Stanton to start the second half.

That decision left the Spartan locker room divided between Stanton and Dowdell; a part of the squad felt that as a senior Dowdell deserved an extended look.

Stanton's play earned him the starting nod the next week at Indiana, but the "Drew Stanton Era began with a resounding thud." He played so badly he assumed he would be benched.

But something interesting happened in the locker room at half-time. Stanton stood up and apologized to his teammates for his lousy play, praised his offensive line, and promised he would turn it around in the second half.

He did. He ran for 134 yards, completed some big passes, and led the Spartans to a 30-20 comeback win that had State fans chanting his name. The starting job was his, and Stanton went on to a stellar career. He still remains the school's all-time leader in completion percentage and is third in career passing yardage.

Courtesy, forthrightness, our sense of justice, and our Christ-centered desire to repair the damage to a relationship demand apologies from us sometime. We may apologize when we bump into someone or are uncharacteristically harsh or cruel.

But too many Christians in the increasingly hostile environment that is contemporary America find themselves apologizing for their faith and the temerity they display in inviting someone to church or saying the name of Jesus in their presence. We shouldn't. To apologize for our faith is to declare in effect that we are ashamed of Jesus.

Like Peter and John, we do not have to tell anyone we're sorry for our faith or abashedly try to excuse our actions in the name of Christ. We are Christians, heart and soul. And don't those who purposely flaunt their behavior in Christians' faces tell us, "If you don't like it, live with it"? We're just doing the same. Only in our case, we're talking about living eternally.

I thought that was great of him.
    — *Center Chris Morris on Drew Stanton's halftime apology*

We should never apologize for Jesus.

REGRETS, ANYONE?

Read 2 Corinthians 7:8-13.

"Godly sorrow brings repentance that leads to salvation and leaves no regret" (v. 10).

One of Michigan State's greatest multi-sport athletes completed his Spartan career with one major regret.

As a senior in 1972, Brad Van Pelt was officially declared the best college football player in America when he won the Maxwell Award. He was the first defensive back to win it. From 1970-72 at Michigan State, Van Pelt "was a terror on the football field." He was, in fact, "an athletic anomaly." In an age when players were smaller than they are today, here he was, a fearsome safety who stood 6-foot-5 and weighed 220 lbs.

He was an All-American his last two seasons as a Spartan and was a team captain in 1972. Decades after he last played for the Spartans, he remains tied for fourth among MSU's career leaders with 14 interceptions and second only to Lynn Chandnois in interception return yards. He was inducted into the College Football Hall of Fame in 2001.

Van Pelt was described as "a mammoth athlete, intimidating as a rover back in the secondary or returning kicks." But the gridiron wasn't the only place he dominated. He was a right-handed pitcher for the MSU baseball team, helping them to the Big Ten title in 1971. He was drafted five times by major-league baseball teams. He also starred for three seasons as a power forward on

SPARTANS

the MSU basketball team and had pro potential.

That versatility led to Van Pelt's lone regret about his time at MSU. He won an incredible seven varsity letters before the New York Giants picked him in the second round of the 1973 NFL draft. He signed a contract and went on to a Pro-Bowl career that saw him named as the Giants' Player of the Decade for the 1970s.

That contract resulted in one of the two regrets in Van Pelt's life. As a pro, he was ineligible to play his last seasons at State in basketball and baseball. "I wished I would have waited," he said.

In their classic hit "The Class of '57," the Statler Brothers served up some pure country truth when they sang, "Things get complicated when you get past 18." That complication includes regrets; you have them; so does everyone else: situations and relationships that upon reflection we wish we had handled differently.

Feeling troubled or remorseful over something you've done or left undone is not necessarily a bad thing. That's because God uses regrets to spur us to repentance, which is the decision to change our ways. Repentance in turn is essential to salvation through Jesus Christ. You regret your un-Christlike actions, repent by promising God to mend your ways, and then seek and receive forgiveness for them.

The cold, hard truth is that you will have more regrets in your life. You can know absolutely, however, that you will never ever regret making Jesus the reason for that life.

I would've loved to play those last seasons and earn nine letters.
— Brad Van Pelt on missing his last seasons of basketball and baseball

Regrets are part of living,
but you'll never regret living for Jesus.

DAY 23

WHOLEHEARTEDLY

Read 1 Samuel 13:1-14.

"The Lord has sought out a man after his own heart" (v. 14).

Spartan head coach Suzy Merchant didn't really realize what she was getting when she landed Tori Jankoska. That's because she had no way to measure the size and depth of Jankoska's heart, that literal organ that tried to kill her early on.

Jankoska sits atop a list of Michigan State's greatest women's basketball players that includes Kisha Kelley (Simpson), Lindsay Bowen, Kristin Haynie, Liz Shimek, Alyssa DeHaan, Kalisha Keane, and Aeriel Powers. She finished her career in 2017 as the only women's player in Spartan history to score more than 2,000 points. She set the women's record for career 3-pointers and for career free throws. On Jan. 10, 2017, she set the program's single-game record with 42 points in a 94-75 defeat of Ohio State.

Jankoska wasn't an obvious choice for collegiate basketball stardom. Early on, Merchant considered her to be at best "a very good player" who could do little more than shoot 3-pointers. "I didn't expect her to be a great player," the veteran coach said.

After all, Jankoska wasn't even an obvious choice to live. She was born with a hole in her heart that left her fighting for her life. From that battle, say Merchant and Jankoska's mom, Lisa, came the fighting spirit and heart that carried her to excellence.

She played basketball on a fourth-grade team while she was

still in kindergarten. She was 8 or 9 when her mom signed her up for an MSU basketball camp. Then-head coach Joanne McCallie told Tori's mom she was too small to keep up. She told Lisa to stay the first day, so she could take her daughter home. Needless to say, Tori stayed; her mom never had to again.

Kankoska brought that same fire and heart to MSU. Merchant admitted she was wrong about her superstar because "I didn't know what her work ethic was. . . . She's in the gym all the time." In other words, she gave her heart and her all to become great. "What a champion and what a winner that kid is," Merchant said.

As Tori Kankoska did at Michigan State, we all face defeat. Even though we fight with all we have, we lose sometimes.

At some time, you probably have admitted you were whipped no matter how much it hurt. Always in your life, though, you have known that you would fight for some things with all your heart and never give them up: your family, your country, your friends, your core beliefs.

God should be on that list too. God seeks men and women who will never turn their back on him because they are people after God's own heart. That is, they will never betray God with their unbelief; they will never lose their childlike trust in God; they will never cease to love God with all their heart; they will never fail to number themselves among God's champions.

They are lifetime members of God's team; it's a mighty good one to be on, but it takes heart.

Her heart is bigger than anything.
— *Suzy Merchant on Tori Jankoska*

To be on God's team requires a champion's heart.

DAY 24

UNBELIEVABLE!

Read Hebrews 3:7-19.

"See to it, brothers, that none of you has a sinful, unbelieving heart that turns away from the living God" (v. 12).

Michigan State's undefeated season was history, over and done with. And then, "Something unbelievable happened."

On Oct. 17, 2015, the 7th-ranked Spartans and the 12th-ranked Wolverines collided in an epic showdown. Even before that "something unbelievable," the game lived up to its hype. State moved up and down the field all afternoon against the nation's top-rated defense with quarterback Connor Cook throwing for 328 yards and a touchdown. But the Wolverines always had an answer.

With 1:47 left, Michigan took over on downs at its own 45 with a 23-21 lead. The Wolverines ran the clock down to ten seconds and lined up for a game-ending punt. State didn't send anybody back deep; all U-M had to do to win was get the kick off.

Unbelievably, the Wolverine punter bobbled a low snap. As he scrambled to get the punt away, Spartans swarmed all over him and the ball popped free. Still unbelievably, it landed in the arms of Jalen Watts-Jackson, a redshirt freshman defensive back. Most unbelievably of all, Watts-Jackson ran it into the end zone for a 27-23 win. He thus went in one play "from total obscurity to pulling off one of the most unlikely endings in college football."

"You go from 10 seconds, a guy punting the ball, you're thinking

OK this is done," said State head coach Mark Dantonio. "And then all of a sudden, life gets flipped upside down."

Making the play even more surreal: Watts-Jackson suffered a dislocated hip after teammates piled on him in the end zone; a fan in the stands suffered a heart attack; it was Watts-Jackson's first college touchdown; it was the only time State was ahead.

Much of what taxes the limits of our belief system has little serious, direct effect on our daily lives (except for unbelievable State TDs). Maybe we don't believe in UFOs, Sasquatch, or the viability of electric cars. A healthy dose of skepticism is a natural defense mechanism that helps protect us in a world that all too often has designs on taking advantage of us.

That's not the case, however, when Jesus and God are part of the mix. Quite unbelievably, we often hear people blithely assert they don't believe in God. Or brazenly declare they believe in God but don't believe Jesus was anything but a good man and a great teacher.

All that may sound cool to the smug speaker and his audience. But it's not; it's dangerous. That's because a loving and broken-hearted God awards scoffers the just deserts of their unbelief: banishment from the Promised Land, which isn't a country in the Middle East but is Heaven itself.

Given that scenario, it's downright unbelievable that anyone would not believe.

It can't be true.
— U-M defensive tackle Willie Henry on the unbelievable ending

Perhaps nothing is as unbelievable as that some people insist on not believing in God or his son.

DAY 25

HOMEBODIES

Read John 14:1-6.

"[I]f I go and prepare a place for you, I will come back and take you to be with me" (v 3).

After years of dreaming and trying, George Perles came home.

Perles played football at Michigan State (his career cut short by a knee injury), graduated from there, met his wife there, and had two of his children born in East Lansing. From the first day he came home from serving in the Army and walked onto the campus, his dream was to be Michigan State's head coach.

He served as Duffy Daugherty's defensive line coach until 1972 when he took the same job with the Pittsburgh Steelers. At that point, "Pro football was George Perles' business, but Michigan State was his passion."

His first crack at the head coach's job came in 1976, but his interview turned out to be a mere courtesy. When the State job came open again in 1980, Perles became the clear frontrunner in the eyes of the media and the public before he had even been contacted about it. After he interviewed with athletic director Doug Weaver, "There seemed to be no other serious candidates. . . . It was clear to everyone — even to a husband and wife back in Pittsburgh — that Perles would be named."

He wasn't. In what for Perles was a shocking and crushing disappointment, Frank "Muddy" Waters got the job. Perles reacted gracefully even though he was stunned. How could the job "he wanted so badly [be] pulled away so cruelly?"

Daugherty told Perles he should be glad he didn't get the job right then, that no one could win at Michigan State because of the way probation had depleted the squad. "Next time around, it'll come your way," he said. The veteran head coach was right. After the 1982 season, Waters was fired and George Perles came home to East Lansing as the Spartans' head football coach.

As it was with George Perles, home is not necessarily a matter of geography. It may be that place you share with your family, whether it's in Michigan or Alaska. Or you may feel at home when you return to East Lansing, wondering why you were so eager to leave in the first place. Maybe the home you grew up in still feels like an old shoe, a little worn but comfortable and inviting.

It is no mere happenstance that among the circumstances of life that we most abhor is that of being rootless. That dread results from the sense of home God planted in us. Our God is a God of place, and our place is with him.

Thus, we may live a few blocks away from our parents and grandparents or we may relocate every few years, but we will still sometimes feel as though we don't really belong no matter where we are. We don't; our true home is with God in the place Jesus has gone ahead to prepare for us. We are homebodies and we are perpetually homesick.

[George] Perles would trade all [his] Super Bowl rings and diamonds
for a chance to go back to Michigan State as head coach.
— Sportswriter Lynn Henning

We are continually homesick for our real home,
which is with God in Heaven.

DAY 26

IMPRESS ME!

Read John 1:1-18.

"In the beginning was the Word, and the Word was with God, and the Word was God. . . . The Word became flesh and made his dwelling among us" (vv. 1, 14).

Kirk Gibson was eager to make a good impression on Michigan State's baseball coach. He certainly did that.

Gibson was already a star on the gridiron (See Devotion No. 66.) when MSU's Danny Litwhiler approached him about giving baseball a try. In the fall of 1977, several of his players familiar with Gibson had told the coach the big receiver could help.

When Litwhiler got the chance to speak to Gibson, he went right to the point: "Gibby, why don't you come out for baseball?" "I've been thinking about it" Gibson replied. "Well, don't think about it," the coach said. "Come out."

Litwhiler approached head football coach Darryl Rogers, who was enthusiastic about the idea. He had always encouraged his players who had the talent to try other sports. "I want him back in the fall," the head Spartan warned.

Two months later, Gibson was in the indoor arena with a bat in his hands. From his first swing, "Litwhiler was floored."

Among the contraptions he used, Litwhiler had a tire hanging from a swivel to give his hitters a consistent target to work their stroke into a groove. In his first turn, Gibson "was so pulverizing the tire that steel bands and wires were flying around the gym."

SPARTANS

It got better when Mike Marshall, the National League Cy Young winner in 1974, stopped by practice and agreed to throw to the hitters. He was at State working on his doctorate. Gibson continued to impress. Right away, he sent a pitch into the netting that would have been a home run at Kobs Field.

In his lone, impressive season with the baseball team, Gibson hit .390 with a school-record 16 home runs and was All-America.

That eye-catching person at the office. A job search complete with interview. A class reunion. The new neighbors. We are constantly about the fraught task of wanting to make an impression on people. We want them to remember us, obviously in a flattering way, which means we perhaps should be circumspect in our personal conduct.

We make that impression, good or bad, generally in two ways. Even with instant communication on the Internet — perhaps especially with the Internet — we primarily influence the opinion others have of us by our words. After that, we can advance to the next level by making an impression with our actions.

God gave us an impression of himself in exactly the same way. In Jesus, God took the unprecedented step of appearing to mortals as one of us, as mere flesh and bone. We now know for all time the sorts of things God does and the sorts of things God says. In Jesus, God put his divine foot forward to make a good impression on each one of us.

Boy, he has a good swing.
— *Mike Marshall's first impression of Kirk Gibson*

Through Jesus' words and actions,
God seeks to impress us with his love.

FIREPROOF

Read Malachi 3:1-5.

*"Who can endure the day of his coming? Who can stand
when he appears? For he will be like a refiner's fire or a
launderer's soap. He will sit as a refiner and purifier of
silver" (vv. 2, 3a).*

The celebration of what was called "among the biggest upsets in
all college football history" included the burning down of a "very
ugly, unacademic structure" on campus.

From 1911-15, head football coach John F. Macklin produced
what is still the best winning record in Michigan State gridiron
history. He posted an .853 percentage with a record of 29-5. In
1913, Macklin "sensed that now the time was at hand" for the
school's first-ever defeat of Michigan.

The hard-driving coach scrimmaged his team to exhaustion
the week of the game, installing electric lights for work after dark.
"We would be too tired to eat even," declared Herb Straight, a
three-time letter-winning lineman (1914-16).

All the hard work paid off. On Oct. 18, Michigan Agricultural
College beat the Wolverines 12-7. Carp Julian and Hewitt Miller
scored the two MAC touchdowns. Quarterback George Gauthier
completed seven of 19 passes for 100 yards, "a phenomenal performance with the fat ball of those days."

A wild celebration ensued, including the inevitable bonfire
and student snake-dancing. A fire on Sunday destroyed the barn

of the Agriculture Board's secretary, which stood near the present Student Union building. Few regretted the loss of the unsightly building. Defective wiring was suggested, but no one ever came up with a satisfactory explanation for how the fire started.

The cow housed in the barn was unharmed; she had been led to meet the trainload of students returning from Ann Arbor.

The vast majority of us never face the horror and agony of being badly burned. For most of us, fire conjures up images of romantic evenings before a fireplace, fond memories of hot dogs, marshmallows, and ghost stories around a campfire, or rib eyes sizzling on a grill. Fire is an absolutely necessary tool.

Yet we appreciate that fire also has the capacity to destroy. The Bible reflects fire's dual nature, using it to describe almighty God himself and as a metaphor for both punishment and purification. God appeared to Moses in a burning bush and led the wandering Israelites by night as a pillar of fire. Malachi describes Jesus as a purifying and refining fire. Fire is also the ultimate symbol for the destructive force of God's wrath, a side to God we quite understandably prefer not to dwell upon. Our sin and disobedience, though, do not only break God's heart but also anger him.

Thus, fire in the Bible is basically a symbol for God's holiness. Whether that holiness destroys us or purifies us is the choice we make in our response to Jesus. We are, all of us, tested by fire.

No one said so, but it appeared the fire was part of the victory celebration.
— Former Michigan State SID Fred Stabley in The Spartans

God's holy fire is either the total destroyer or the ultimate purifier; we are fireproof only in Jesus.

LESSON LEARNED

Read Psalm 143.

"Teach me to do your will, for you are my God" (v. 10).

Shilique Calhoun had a lot to learn. As it turned out, he was a very good student.

As he grew up, Calhoun was interested in basketball, not football. A persistent Joe Trezza, the head football coach, convinced Calhoun to try the sport for a week. The 6'2" eighth grader towered above everyone else, but he knew nothing about football.

So the learning process began. Each fall Calhoun showed up for practice, played a variety of positions, and then returned to basketball. When a few recruiters showed up and asked who was looking at Calhoun, Trezza couldn't help but laugh. "He didn't know anything about football," the coach said.

But State defensive coordinator Pat Narduzzi spotted Calhoun his junior season and determined the raw youngster had the size and the character to make him worth the risk of a scholarship. "A fun-loving kid that you love to coach," Narduzzi said of him.

So Calhoun arrived in East Lansing in 2011, and the coaches couldn't figure out where to play him. He wanted to play both offense and defense. Head coach Mark Dantonio had the final say: Calhoun would be a defensive end, a third-down rusher who could also drop back into pass coverage.

There were two problems with that decision: Calhoun was "woefully skinny and did not yet know the intricacies of the posi-

SPARTANS

tion, typically a recipe for disaster in the Big Ten." In his early practices, Calhoun kept trying to bust through the middle of the line only to have his thin self consistently wind up on his backside.

But the coaches kept teaching and Calhoun kept learning. He also gained some weight. He left MSU after his senior season as a three-time first-team All-Big Ten selection and a three-time Second-Team All-American. He was drafted by Oakland in 2016.

Learning about anything in life — including football — requires a combination of education and experience. Education is the accumulation of facts that we call knowledge; experience is the acquisition of wisdom and discernment, which add both purpose and understanding to our knowledge. Education without experience just doesn't have much practical value in our world today.

The most difficult way to learn is trial and error: just dive in blindly and mess up. Better luck next time. The best way to learn is through example coupled with a set of instructions. With this process, someone has gone ahead to show you the way and has written down all the information you need to follow.

In teaching us the way to live godly lives, God chose the latter method. He set down in his book the habits, actions, and attitudes that make for a way of life in accordance with his wishes. He also sent us Jesus to explain and to illustrate.

God teaches us not only how to exist but how to live. We just need to be attentive students.

He does what [the coaches] tell him to do because he's a fast learner.
— Shilique Calhoun's mom, Cynthia Mimes, before MSU's 2014 season

To learn from Jesus is to learn what life is all about and how God means for us to live it.

DAY 29

A HELPING HAND

Read Psalm 121.

"My help comes from the Lord, the maker of heaven and earth" (v. 2).

Spartan head football coach Biggie Munn once got some un-expected help during a game: A fan clambered down from the stands to offer him a suggestion about what play to run.

Clarence "Biggie" Munn coached the Spartans from 1947-53 to a remarkable 54-9-2 record. His 1952 team won the national championship. His 1953 squad won the Big Ten title in its first year of competition in the league and beat UCLA in the Rose Bowl. He then retired from coaching to assume duties as MSU's athletic director, a position he held until 1971.

The football team annually hands out the "Biggie Munn Award" to the squad's most motivational player. Munn was inducted into the College Football Hall of Fame in 1959. In in 1961, he became State's first inductee into the Michigan Sports Hall of Fame.

From 1950-53, Munn's Spartans went 36-2-0, including a 28-game win streak, in the most glorious four-season run in State football history. The 1951 squad went 9-0-0 and opened the season with wins over Oregon State, Michigan, and Ohio State.

After that herculean pair of wins over the Wolverines and the Buckeyes, however, the Spartans found themselves in trouble against Marquette, trailing 14-6 in the fourth quarter. That's when Munn felt a tap on his shoulder and turned to face an excited fan.

"Wise up, Biggie," he said. "You need a quick touchdown. [Have quarterback Al] Dorow throw a long pass to [sophomore halfback Billy] Wells." Security officers then escorted the fan back to his seat before the coach could reply.

Munn didn't call the play, but sure enough, a play or two later, Dorow hit Wells with a bomb that went for a touchdown. "My friend was back at once," Munn said. "'That's the boy, Biggie,' he said. 'But you're on your own now. I'm due on the swing shift down at Oldsmobile.'" The Spartans rallied for a 20-14 win.

As do the Spartans in a tightly contested game, we have our ups and downs. Sometimes — often more than once in the journey that is our life — we get to a point when our own resources won't get us through. We need help.

But where to turn? Family and friends? Counselors? Even a pastor? They're certainly better options than the likes of drugs or alcohol. But they're fallible people, and the truth is they sometimes let us down. They simply, for whatever reason, can't or won't always provide what we need.

They're derivative anyway; that is, they were all created. The answer for meaningful, life-changing help that will never fail is the Source: Almighty God. God cares for his people, each one of us. The creator of the cosmos cares about you. He knows you by name and knows exactly what's going on in your life. And he has the power and the desire to help — as no one or nothing else can.

Apparently he had stepped out of the stands to visit with me.
— Biggie Munn on the fan who offered his help in the Marquette game

"May I help you?" isn't just for a store; it's a
question God will ask if you turn to him.

THE SPARTAN WAY

Read Romans 13:8-14.

"The night is nearly over; the day is almost here. So let us put aside the deeds of darkness and put on the armor of light" (v. 12).

Across the years, it has become known as The Spartan Way.

Magic Johnson still does it. Steve Smith did it for Mateen Cleaves. Cleaves did it for Travis Walton. Walton did it for Draymond Green. During the 2015-16 season, Green did it for Denzel Valentine as he became an All-American and the first MSU player to be named the National Player of the Year.

"It" is seizing the mantle of leadership as a Spartan basketball player and then not being done when your playing days are over. You stay in contact with the Spartans and with the next designated leader in particular.

It starts with Johnson. Through his NBA career and beyond, the "everyman sort of legend" has stayed "available and accessible" to the Spartan players. He shows up at games, and frequently when he's in Lansing, he pops by practice. "Who wants to watch practice?" Spartan head coach Tom Izzo once asked. "But he does."

After Valentine laid a triple-double on Kansas on Nov. 17, 2015, only the fourth Spartan to pull off the feat, athletic director Mark Hollis called him to a phone. It was Johnson with congratulations, and it was The Spartan Way at work: "If someone like Magic Johnson can make time for the Spartans, surely everyone else can."

"Your time here is never up," is the way Cleaves has described it. Your playing days may be over, but you're not done. "You keep talking to the guys who come after you. It's what we do. It's why we are who we are."

The Spartan Way has become such a part of the fabric of the basketball program that Cleaves said players now aspire to be the guy in charge. "They want to be in the fraternity, at the table with the big dogs."

It is, after all, The Spartan Way.

You have a way of life that defines and describes you. You're a die-hard Michigan State fan for starters. Maybe you're married with a family. A city guy or a small-town gal. You wear jeans or a suit to work every day. And then there's your faith.

For the Christian, following Jesus more than anything else defines for the world your way of life. It's basically simple in its concept even if it is downright daunting in its execution. You act toward others in a way that would not embarrass you were your day to be broadcast on *Fox News*. You think about others in a way that would not humiliate you should your thoughts be the plotline for a new *CBS* sitcom.

You make your actions and thoughts those of love: at all times, in all things, toward all people. It's the Jesus way of life, and it's the way to life forever with God.

Michigan State bequeaths its leadership like a family heirloom, and ex-players not only pass the torch but also ensure it remains properly lit.
— ESPN's Dana O'Neil on The Spartan Way

**To live the Jesus way is to act with love at all times,
in all things, and toward all people.**

PAY YOUR RESPECTS

Read Mark 8:31-38.

"He then began to teach them that the Son of Man must suffer many things and be rejected by the elders, chief priests and teachers of the law, and that he must be killed" (v. 31).

The Wolverines showed the Spartans such a complete lack of respect that their head coach apologized for what they did. MSU just used it as incentive to blow them out of the stadium.

In the 2014 match-up of the old rivals, the Michigan players jammed a stake into the Spartan Stadium turf before the kickoff. The show of disrespect didn't sit well with Spartan head coach Mark Dantonio and his players. *ESPN* writer Ryan McGee said the action was about as dumb as "walking into a biker bar and telling someone to step outside while wearing Bermuda shorts and sandals with socks."

The results were predictable. The 8th-ranked Spartans wiped up the staked-out turf with the Wolverines, coasting to a 35-11 win. Senior Jeremy Langford ran for 177 yards and three touchdowns, and Connor Cook threw a 70-yard touchdown pass to All-Big Ten wide receiver Tony Lippett to pace the win. State led 14-3 at the break and never looked back.

Until the last minute of the game, that is. Rather than take a knee with a 28-11 lead, the Spartans scored a touchdown on a 1-yard Langford run. Dantonio pulled no punches about why his team did it. "It just felt like we needed to put a stake in them at that point," he said.

The Sunday morning after the game, Wolverine head coach Brady Hoke issued a statement apologizing for the incident, calling it "poor sportsmanship." The show of disrespect was certainly rather misplaced since Michigan went into the game with a 3-4 record and had lost four out of the past five game in the series.

Rodney Dangerfield made a good living with a comedic repertoire that was basically only countless variations on one punch line: "I don't get no respect." Dangerfield was successful because he struck a chord with his audience. Like the late comedian, we all seek a measure of respect in our lives. We want the respect, the esteem, and the regard we feel we have earned.

The truth is, though, that more often than not we don't get it. We often find ourselves put down or ignored. But more often than not we don't get it. Still, we shouldn't feel too badly; we're in good company. In the ultimate example of disrespect, Jesus — God in the flesh — was treated as the worst type of criminal. He was arrested, bound, scorned, ridiculed, spit upon, tortured, condemned, and executed.

God allowed his son to undergo such treatment because of his high regard and his love for each one of us. We are respected by almighty God! Could anyone else's respect really matter?

They disrespected us right out of the gate. We weren't having that.
— Connor Cook on Michigan's stake-planting

**You may not get the respect you deserve,
but at least nobody's spitting on you
and driving nails into you as they did to Jesus.**

DAY 32

DRY RUN

Read John 4:1-26.

*"Everyone who drinks this water will be thirsty again,
but whoever drinks the water I give him will never thirst.
Indeed, the water I give him will become in him a spring
of water welling up to eternal life" (vv. 13-14).*

Not even a wrong call by the replay official could keep the Spartans from breaking a six-year drought against the Wolverines.

When the Spartans trotted into the Big House on Oct. 25, 2008, they had not beaten Michigan since 2001. They had not won in Ann Arbor since 1990. This was the year, though, that the dismal streak was to end. As *ESPN*'s Adam Rittenberg put it, "The Spartans are superior on both sides of the ball. They have more experience. They have more familiarity with their head coach."

But MSU linebacker Adam Decker was aware that many fans were bracing for "a typical Spartan slide" after a loss to Ohio State the week before. He admitted fans and the media had "no reason not to say that until we give them a reason to prove them wrong."

The Spartans gave them a reason. After falling behind 21-14 in the third quarter, they scored 21 unanswered points to win 35-21. All-American Javon Ringer rushed for 194 yards and two scores, and senior quarterback Brian Hoyer was 17-of-29 passing for 282 yards and a season-high three touchdowns. For the game, the MSU offense rolled up 473 yards.

The Spartans won despite being the victims of a call so bad

SPARTANS

that Big Ten Commissioner Jim Delany called it "a mistake of an application of a rule" and declared discipline could follow. In the first quarter, the officials correctly disallowed a U-M touchdown when the receiver came down on the pylon. In apparent ignorance of a clear rule, the replay official awarded a touchdown.

It didn't matter. The blown call slowed the Spartans down, but it couldn't stop them from ending the drought and gathering in a corner of the Big House to raucously celebrate with their fans.

You can walk across that river you boated on in the spring. The city's put all neighborhoods on water restriction. That beautiful lawn you fertilized and seeded will turn a sickly, pale green and may lapse all the way to brown. Somebody wrote "Wash Me" on the rear window of your truck; you didn't think it was very funny.

The sun bakes everything, including the concrete. The earth itself seems exhausted, just barely hanging on. It's a drought.

It's the way a soul that shuts God out looks.

God instilled the physical sensation of thirst in us to warn us of our body's need for water. He also gave us a spiritual thirst that can be quenched only by his presence in our lives. Without God, we are like tumbleweeds, dried out and windblown, offering the illusion of life where there is only death.

Living water — the water of life — is readily available in Jesus. We may drink our fill, and thus we slake our thirst and end our soul's drought — forever.

This one counts as more than one. We took a step forward toward changing the culture in this state.
— Mark Dantonio on the importance of ending the drought vs U-M

Our soul thirsts for God's refreshing presence.

DAY 33

THE NIGHTMARE

Read Mark 5:1-20.

"What do you want with me, Jesus, Son of the Most High God? Swear to God that you won't torture me!" (v. 7)

State head coach Nick Saban talked about nightmares. Weeks later, Michigan lived one.

During the last week of August 1999, only a few days before the season opener against Oregon, Saban asked his team, "In all the horror movies you've seen, who is the scariest character?" The players conferred until someone nominated Freddy Krueger, the stuff of everyone's nightmares from the *Nightmare on Elm Street* series. The suggestion drew nods of approval.

"Why him?" Saban asked. "He'll get you when you're awake," answered defensive end Robaire Smith. "He'll get you in your dreams. You can't go to sleep on Freddy Krueger." Saban was ready: "He doesn't quit, does he? He's relentless. We have to be relentless, just like Freddy Krueger." And on Oct. 9, they were, in the process becoming the stuff of Michigan's worst nightmare.

The Wolverines went into the game a heady 5-0 with a lofty No.-3 ranking. State showed up 5-0 and ranked 11th. When it was all over, Michigan left town with a 34-31 loss, two meaningless Wolverine touchdowns in the fourth quarter disguising the fact that the game was a rout.

The relentless State defense was the scariest part of the day. It held the Wolverines to six yards rushing "and mauled them from

SPARTANS

the start." "They knew it was over when it was 7-0, the way we were beating them up," declared cornerback Amp Campbell.

The Spartan offense was just as scary. Quarterback Bill Burke threw for a school-record 400 yards. Wide receiver Plaxico Burress terrorized the Michigan secondary with ten receptions for 255 yards, which broke Andre Rison's school record.

For State fans, the game was a sweet dream. For the Wolverine faithful, the whole thing was one long, awful nightmare.

Falling. Drowning. Standing naked in a room crowded with fully dressed people. They're nightmares, dreams that jolt us from our sleep in anxiety or downright terror. The film industry has used our common nightmares to create horror movies that allow us to experience our fears vicariously. This includes the formulaic "evil vs. good" movies in which demons and the like render good virtually helpless in the face of their power and ruthlessness.

The spiritual truth, though, is that it is evil that has come face to face with its worst nightmare in Jesus. We seem to understand that our basic mission as Jesus' followers is to further his kingdom and change the world through emulating him in the way we live and love others. But do we appreciate that in truly living for Jesus, we are daily tormenting the very devil himself?

Satan and his lackeys quake helplessly in fear before the power of almighty God that is in us through Jesus.

[Nick] Saban's [nightmare] ploy was effective. Ask Michigan, which lived a nightmare of its own Saturday in East Lansing.
— Sports Illustrated's Tim Layden on the 1999 MSU-Michigan game

**As the followers of Jesus Christ,
we are the stuff of Satan's nightmares.**

DAY 34

TO BOLDLY GO

Read 1 Peter 3:13-22.

"Always be prepared to give an answer to everyone who asks you to give the reason for the hope that you have" (v. 15a).

Vern Payne realized he had to do something different and at least slightly bold to land the prized recruit he was pursuing. So he drove down to Hardee's and ordered a Coca-Cola.

In 1975, Payne was an assistant basketball coach at Michigan State in charge of recruiting. One of his targets the spring of that year was Gregory Kelser, who has been called "the best player, that wasn't a guard, in the history of MSU's program." He was a first-team All-America as a senior in 1979 and was the first Big Ten player to rack up more than 2,000 points and 1,000 rebounds in a career. He is the only Michigan State player to accomplish the feat and remains fourth on the Spartans' career scoring list.

Payne was such an ace recruiter that he landed Kelser's signature on a letter of intent before he ever visited the Michigan State campus. But that doesn't mean Kelser was a sure thing to wear green and white and help win two Big Ten titles and a national championship. His first visit his senior year of high school was to Minnesota. He wasn't even being recruited by Michigan State until a Christmas tournament his senior season. Payne showed up to scout another player, but it was Kelser who played so well he shot to the top of the coach's wish list.

SPARTANS

The competition for Kelser became fierce in the spring of '75. On signing day, Payne pulled up to Kelser's home to see cars all over the place. Representatives from Arizona State, Central Michigan, and Detroit were inside with full scholarships in hand. They were waiting for Kelser to come home from work.

Payne boldly decided not to wait and never got out of his car. Instead, he drove to the local Hardee's where Kelser was working behind the counter and placed his order: "I'll have a Coke and a signature. . . . The startled Kelser obliged on both accounts."

To act boldly is to take unconventional action that involves an element of risk. We all at times in our lives act boldly. When you proposed marriage, for example. Or when you took that new job. We act boldly because we believe the reward justifies the risk.

Why is it then that so many of us who are confident and bold in our professional and personal lives are such timid little things when it comes to our faith life? Why are we so afraid to speak boldly of and act boldly for Jesus? Do we fear offending someone? Are we afraid of rejection? And yet we allegedly serve a Lord who went out of his way to offend the religious authorities and who ultimately was rejected unto death. If anything, Jesus was bold.

Our faith should be burning so strongly in us that we cannot help but live boldly for Jesus. After all, how can we expect Jesus to step boldly forward on judgment day and claim us as his own when we don't claim him as our own now?

[Gregory] Kelser didn't charge [Vern] Payne for the Coke.
— *in* Tales of the Magical Spartans

**We serve a Lord bold enough to die for us;
we should at least live boldly for him.**

GET A CLUE

Read Matthew 16:21-23.

"[Y]ou do not have in mind the things of God, but the things of men" (v. 23b).

Logic dictates that if one college coach after another says a kid's not good enough to make it, they are right. In Jack Conklin's case, however, reality dictated that all those coaches were just clueless.

As Jack and his dad, Darren, traveled from camp to camp trying to catch coaches' attention, they became increasingly bewildered. An offensive tackle, Jack performed well at the camps. He was as big as the hotshot recruits, had longer arms, and was faster. Nevertheless, the duo pretty much met with the same response wherever they went. "Coaches said they had no scholarships available. They flocked to more decorated recruits. They thanked Conklin for coming but gave limited or no feedback on his play."

The problem was Jack's hometown of Plainwell, pop. 3,804. When the Spartans took a look at Jack's tape, they saw a dominating tackle. Eighty percent of the team's runs went in his direction. But the tiny high school's competition just wasn't very good.

As MSU offensive line coach Mark Staten said about Conklin, "He's beating the crap out of a guy, but that guy's 5-6 and 140 pounds." Thus, coaches felt they couldn't really gauge how good Jack Conklin was. So they passed him by.

Jack was set to attend a prep school to boost his stock. At the last moment, MSU called. They had a spot for him in the spring of

2012. He would be put on scholarship sometime during the year.

This player coaches were clueless about was a three-year starter for the Spartans. In 2015, he was a first-team All-American, State's first offensive tackle to receive the honor since Flozell Adams in 1997. He was also first-team All-Big Ten, State's first offensive tackle to earn the designation since Sean Poole in 2004.

Clueless. It's one of our age's most venomous insults. It's an interesting word in that it is its own oxymoron. People are clueless only when they do indeed have the clues at hand and still don't get it. It's not to be confused with ignorance, which occurs when people don't have access to facts, figures, and information.

From the desert-dwelling Israelites grumbling about Moses and God to the Pharisees and other religious leaders of Jesus' day, the Bible is replete with the clueless. Simon Peter, who had all the clues he needed standing right in front of his face, drew a soul-searing rebuke from Jesus for being clueless.

The Bible remains relevant and timeless because centuries after it was compiled, human nature hasn't changed one bit. As it was in Jesus' time, people who have heard the Gospel may still be divided into the clued-in and the clueless: those who get it and those who don't. Fortunately for the clueless, they can always change groups as Peter did. They can affirm Jesus as their savior and surrender to him. They just need you to clue them in.

They've looked at him, they've evaluated him, and they flat-out don't think he's good enough.
– Darren Conklin on why clueless coaches didn't offer Jack a scholarship

Clueless or clued-in is a matter of whether
you have given your life to Jesus.

DO WHAT YOU MUST

Read 2 Samuel 12:1-15a.

"The Lord sent Nathan to David" (v. 1).

Sometimes you just gotta do what you gotta do. For Aisha Jefferson that once meant leading the Spartans to a win in the NCAA Tournament while pausing every now and then to throw up.

Jefferson ended her Spartan career in 2010 with 1,194 points, 11th highest in program history, and 652 rebounds, the 12th highest total. She was the fifth player in MSU history to be a three-time captain and shared the team's MVP award her senior season.

Head coach Suzy Merchant once said of Jefferson, "She's just our heart and soul." Never perhaps was that demonstrated more starkly than on March 20, 2010, in the first round of the NCAA Tournament. The Spartans defeated Bowling Green 72-62, which wasn't a surprise since State was a fifth seed and was favored.

What was most remarkable about the game was Jefferson's performance. A forward, she scored 17 points, nabbed nine rebounds, and handed out three assists while not committing a single turnover. So what? The points, rebounds, and assists totals didn't even represent season highs for her.

But she put together that game despite regular visits to the end of the bench to throw up in a trash can. Her stomach was in such bad shape that she had begun vomiting during the team's morning shootaround.

Jefferson was clearly the difference in the game. For most of

SPARTANS

the contest, when she was on the court, the Spartans were physically dominant. When she wasn't, State "looked the worse for it — although not as bad as Jefferson looked with her trash can."

For Jefferson, the stomach problem wasn't anything new, but a condition called gastroparesis, which dated back before the 2009-10 season. She simply battled through it, doing what she had to do to help her team win.

"It was my night," she said. Trash can and all.

Aisha Jefferson certainly didn't want to spend time during a Spartan basketball game bent over and throwing up. But it was the only way she could play. You've also had to do some things in your life that you really didn't want to do. Maybe when you put your daughter on severe restriction, broke the news of a death in the family, fired a friend, or underwent surgery. You plowed ahead because you knew it was for the best or you had no choice.

Nathan certainly didn't want to confront King David and tell him what a miserable reprobate he'd been, but the prophet had no choice: Obedience to God overrode all other factors. Of all that God asks of us in the living of a godly life, obedience is perhaps the most difficult. After all, our history of disobedience stretches all the way back to the Garden of Eden.

The problem is that God expects obedience not only when his wishes match our own but also when they don't. Obedience to God is a way of life, not a matter of convenience.

I had a little stomach issue, but I had a lot of Mylanta.
— Aisha Jefferson on her travails during the Bowling Green game

Obedience requires being ready to do whatever God asks, whatever you must do for him.

DAY 37

WILD AND CRAZY

Read Mark 1:1-11.

"John's clothes were made of camel's hair, and he had a leather belt around his waist. His food was locusts and wild honey" (v. 4).

Though "the result . . . was disappointing to virtually everyone," the hoopla leading up to the legendary 1966 Notre Dame game was as wild and crazy as it could be.

The game of Nov. 19 in Spartan Stadium marked the first time in college football history that the nation's two top-rated teams had squared off that late in the season. Accordingly, anticipation collapsed into hysteria.

ABC declared it had received 50,000 letters demanding the game be shown in all parts of the country, and the NCAA relented and allowed the network to broadcast the game nationally rather than just regionally. The network promoted the game as "the greatest battle since Hector fought Achilles." *ABC* publicity director Beano Cook, who later achieved fame with *ESPN*, remarked that the network had put out enough material "to make *Gone with the Wind* look like a short story."

A Saginaw beer store owner said he was willing to sell his business for four game tickets plus $1,700 for his stock and $4,000 for the store's good will. He was serious enough to advertise his offer in a Detroit newspaper.

The requests for media credentials were unprecedented. More

than 300 writers were assigned to the main press deck. An emergency row of more than eighty seats consisting of stools borrowed from campus laboratories was added. Many reporters still had to stand up in what was believed to be "the largest assemblage [of media personnel] ever to work a college game."

The game itself was tense, but far from wild and crazy. It ended in a 10-10 tie when Notre Dame ran out the clock.

Part of the lure of sports is how the games sometimes lapse into the wild and crazy, such as the hoopla surrounding State's famous (or infamous) 1966 encounter with Notre Dame. But ponder a moment the notion that Jesus calls each one of us to a wild, crazy, and adventuresome life, though perhaps not one as bizarre as that of John the Baptist. If this is true, then why is it that church and faith life quite often seem so boring to many of us? Why don't Christians lead lives of adventure and excitement?

Many do. Heading into the uncharted waters of the mission field is certainly exciting. Helping the homeless turn their lives around isn't dull at all. Neither is working with youth, teaching Sunday school, entering the chaplaincy for the military, or riding with a Christian biker gang.

The truth is we play it safe. We prefer to do what we want to do rather than what God calls us to do. As a result, we pass on the chance to be part of a great adventure story. If we truly follow Jesus, there is nothing common or ordinary about our lives.

The mounting hysteria was incredible.
— Fred W. Stabley on the '66 Notre Dame game

We are a bunch of wild and crazy guys and gals
when we truly surrender our lives to Jesus.

DAY 38

THE PIONEER SPIRIT

Read Luke 5:1-11.

"So they pulled their boats up on shore, left everything and followed him" (v. 11).

Gideon Smith was a pioneer not just for Michigan State but for all of college football.

From 1913-15, Smith was a dominant tackle for Michigan Agricultural College. His teams went 17-3, including the legendary undefeated team of 1913, and were 2-1 against Michigan.

Smith was a transfer student from Ferris College who tried out for the team in 1912. Head coach John Macklin turned him away by refusing to issue him a uniform. Undeterred, Smith reported to practice anyway, wearing high-school gear loaned to him by a classmate. "Impressed by Smith's rugged play," Macklin allowed him to stay on. He was on the varsity in 1913, which made him the first black player in the school's football history and only the third black man to play major college football for any school.

On road trips, Smith couldn't eat or stay with the rest of the team. Macklin would give him some money, and he would find his own accommodations and food. He would then reappear in time for the pregame warmups. During games, Smith endured racially charged verbal abuse from fans everywhere. End Blake Miller said it was the kind of stuff that "couldn't be printed."

Smith was "a run-stuffing defender" that the *Detroit Times* said "had the agility of a cat." When a play came his way, "he folded up the whole side of the opposing line as if he were playing an accordion." In an age when tackles and guards were allowed to carry the ball, Smith occasionally got the ball on "tackle around" plays to make the most of his speed and power.

Smith was the first black man to graduate from MAC. He is a charter member of both the National Football Foundation Hall of Fame and Michigan State's Athletics Hall of Fame.

Going to a place in your life you've never been before requires a willingness to take risks and face uncertainty head-on. You may have never helped make a way for others who came behind you as Gideon Smith did, but you've had your moments when your latent pioneer spirit manifested itself. That time you changed careers, ran a marathon, learned Spanish, or went back to school.

Attempting new things invariably begets apprehension; on the other hand, when life becomes too comfortable and too much of a routine, it gets boring. The same is true of God, who is downright dangerous because he calls us to be anything but comfortable as we serve him.

He summons us to continuously blaze new trails in our faith life, to follow him no matter what. Stepping out on faith is risky all right, but the reward is a life of accomplishment, adventure, and joy that cannot be equaled anywhere else.

The esteem in which the university holds him now is a reflection of the difference he made in the university's story, and the story of so many.
— John Milton Belcher III, grandson of Gideon Smith

**Unsafe and downright dangerous, God calls us
out of the place where we are comfortable to a life
of adventure and trailblazing in his name.**

DAY 39

LIMITED-TIME OFFER

Read Psalm 103.

"As for man, his days are like grass, he flourishes like a flower of the field; the wind blows over it and it is gone. . . . But from everlasting to everlasting the Lord's love is with those who fear him" (vv. 15-17).

Michigan State's men's basketball program was once rocked by the sudden death of its head coach.

In 1965, John Benington was summoned to rescue a program with only one winning record (14-10) in the last six seasons. The hire amounted to a homecoming for Benington, who had served as an assistant coach at MSU from 1950-56.

East Lansing found itself with a man who drew "as much affection from campus and community as any prominent head coach had managed at Michigan State." Benington was in truth a really nice guy. One writer said he "was so considerate that sometimes [his] charity was almost humorous."

Benington's teams won 56 games in his four seasons. His 1966-67 team shared the Big Ten title with Indiana, which got the NCAA tourney bid because it had gone longer without an appearance.

Among the MSU coaches at the time, racquetball was the sport of choice. They often played a game or two at noon before heading to the commissary for some soup. After one set of games in April 1969, Benington had some difficulty breathing. It was later determined he had suffered a heart attack. He recovered quickly and by the summer was jogging and playing golf again.

On Sept. 10, Benington planned to work half a day and then take his car for a tune-up. When he failed to come home by 6 p.m., his daughter called assistant coach Gus Ganakas. He and fellow assistant Bob Nordmann met Benington's wife at Jenison Fieldhouse to look for him.

They found him dead in the shower, the victim of a second, massive heart attack after he had jogged. He was only 47.

A heart attack, cancer, a sudden stroke, or an accident will probably take — or has already taken — someone you know or love who, like John Benington, was "too young to die."

The death of a younger person never seems to "make sense." That's because such a death belies the common view of death as the natural end of a life lived well and lived long. Moreover, you can't see the whole picture as God does, so you can't know how the death furthers God's kingdom.

At such a time, you can seize the comforting truth that God is in control and therefore everything will be all right one day. You can also gain a sense of urgency in your own life by appreciating that God's offer of life through Jesus Christ is a limited-time offer that expires at your death — and there's no guarantee about when that will be.

[John] Benington's death slammed a campus and community aware of the kind of person he was.

— *Lynn Henning in* Spartan Seasons

**God offers you life through Jesus Christ,
but you must accept the offer before your death,
which is when it expires.**

SWEET WORDS

Read Romans 8:28-39.

"In all these things we are more than conquerors through him who loved us" (v. 37).

Clarence "Biggie" Munn was giving serious thought to resigning as State's head football coach until a player delivered him some unexpected affirmation.

Munn's seven-year stint (1947-53) as the Spartans' head coach included a sterling 54-9-2 record, the 1952 national championship, and a 24-game win streak. His career in East Lansing didn't get off to a flying start, however.

Munn's debut as Michigan State College's fourteenth head football coach came against Michigan in Ann Arbor. The head Wolverine wasn't too keen on his former assistant's coaching a rival school in the same state. Munn knew the Michigan coach would do everything he could to embarrass him.

He did. Michigan would win the national championship that season, and the Wolverines ran up the score, winning 55-0. "I almost broke into tears," Munn said. "I could hardly bring myself to go into the locker room and face my boys."

The team rebounded to win its next three games. Against Kentucky, though, George Guerre, the team's star halfback who was inducted into the MSU Athletics Hall of Fame in 2007, broke his leg on a 10-yard touchdown run. State lost 7-6.

Disheartened by the loss of both the game and his star, Munn seriously considered hanging it up. But Michigan State football history was changed at a prep banquet that week at which Guerre joined Munn. Somebody sarcastically asked Guerre, "What kind of guy is this Biggie Munn anyway?" Guerre replied, "Biggie Munn is the kind of a guy you're glad to break a leg for."

Munn overheard Guerre and said to himself, "If a coach can win this kind of respect from players, I'm staying." And so he did.

You make a key decision. All excited, you tell your best friend or spouse and anxiously await a reaction. "Boy, that was dumb" is the answer you get. Or a friend's life spirals out of control into a total disaster. Do you pretend you don't know that messed-up person?

Everybody needs affirmation in some degree. That is, we all occasionally need someone to say something positive about us, that we are worth something, and that God loves us.

The follower of Jesus does what our Lord did when he encountered someone whose life was a mess. Rather than seeing what they were, he saw what they could become. Life is hard; it breaks us all to some degree. To be like Jesus, we see past the problems of the broken and the hurting and envision their potential, understanding that not condemning is not condoning.

The Christian's words of affirmation are the greatest and most joyous of all. They constitute a message of victory and triumph from which nothing can separate us or defeat us.

I give George Guerre credit for keeping me in coaching.
— *Clarence 'Biggie' Munn*

**The greatest way to affirm lost persons
is to lead them to Christ.**

DAY 41

RUN FOR IT

Read John 20:1-10.

"Peter and the other disciple started for the tomb. Both were running, but the other disciple outran Peter and reached the tomb first" (vv. 3-4).

In a game that could propel Michigan State to the Rose Bowl, Lorenzo White ran and ran and ran — and ran some more.

The passing of four decades has never eclipsed the fact that White is the greatest running back in MSU history. From 1984-87, he rushed for 4,887 yards, still the school record. He also holds the Spartan records for career attempts (1,082), rushing touchdowns (43), and yards rushing in a season (2,066 in 1985). He was a two-time All-America.

When George Perles took over the State football program in 1983, he asked the Spartan faithful to give him five seasons to turn around a program that had been 10-23 in the three seasons prior to his arrival. Thus, the pressure was on in 1987.

This was the season of the "Gang Green" defense, and it all led to "the most anticipated sporting event on the MSU campus in years." It was a showdown on Nov. 14 between the 13th-ranked Spartans and 16th-ranked Indiana for the Big Ten championship.

As it turned out, "the Hoosiers had no chance" in the 27-3 cakewalk as Perles unleashed White on them. He ran the ball an astounding 56 times, which set a school record (that still stands). The fans kept him from tying or breaking the NCAA record of 57 carries. With time still on the clock, they rushed the field, forcing an early halt to the game.

At one point, Perles told White, "I want you to break every record in the book," so he kept giving the ball to his senior star long after the outcome had been decided. Perles' aim was to help White's chances for the Heisman Trophy. (He finished fourth).

The coach once asked White if he were tired. When the running back said he wasn't, Perles said, "You're a liar, but I'm gonna give you the ball anyway." He did and White kept running.

Hit the ground running — every morning that's what you do as you leave the house and re-enter the rat race. You run errands; you run though a presentation; you give someone a run for his money; you always want to be in the running and never run-of-the-mill.

You're always running toward something, such as your goals, or away from something, such as your past. Many of us spend much of our lives foolhardily attempting to run away from God, the purposes he has for us, and the blessings he waits to give us.

No matter how hard or how far you run, though, you can never outrun yourself or God. God keeps pace with you, calling you in the short run to take care of the long run by falling to your knees and running for your life — to Jesus — just as Peter and the other disciple ran that first Easter morning.

On your knees, you run all the way to glory.

The adrenaline was pumping so hard I didn't feel it. But after that game? I had cramps in my sleep all night.
— Lorenzo White after the '87 Indiana game

You can run to eternity by going to your knees.

DAY 42

SURPRISE ME!

Read 1 Thessalonians 5:1-11.

"But you, brothers, are not in darkness so that this day should surprise you like a thief" (v. 4).

Aaron Bates reacted as though the call were no surprise. He was the only one.

On Sept. 18, 2010, Michigan State and Notre Dame put on an old-fashioned barnburner. A pedestrian first half that ended in a 7-7 tie gave little hint of the excitement that was to come.

Early in the third quarter, sophomore Edwin Baker broke off a 56-yard touchdown run, but Notre Dame answered with a score of its own. Freshman Le'Veon Bell, who had 114 yards rushing for the day, put the Spartans back in the lead with a 16-yard scoring run. This time the Irish responded with a pair of touchdowns to lead 28-21 with 12:30 to play.

A 24-yard pass from quarterback Kirk Cousins to junior wide receiver B.J. Cunningham forged a 28-28 tie at the 7:43 mark. After neither team could break the deadlock, Notre Dame kicked a field goal on its initial possession of overtime to lead 31-28..

When the Spartans did nothing with their three downs, the team lined up for the obvious game-tying field goal that would force a second overtime. To practically everyone's surprise, the kick never came. Instead, the coaches called for a fake with head coach Mark Dantonio delivering the news to Bates.

The senior kicker reacted to the surprising call casually, but he had a surprise waiting for him: the play didn't go as planned. Bell was to get the ball, but he ran into a pair of Notre Dame players. The collision left senior tight end Charlie Gantt open.

A former high school quarterback, Bates calmly escaped from a pack of chasing defenders, spotted Gantt, and hit him with a 29-yard touchdown pass. State suddenly had a 34-31 win. Even Irish head coach Brian Kelly admitted he was shocked by the call.

Surprise birthday parties are a delight. What's the fun of opening Christmas presents when we already know what's in them? Some surprises in life (such as a sudden win over Notre Dame) provide us with experiences that are both joyful and delightful.

Generally, though, we expend energy and resources to avoid most surprises and the impact they may have upon our lives. We may be surprised by the exact timing of a baby's arrival, but we nevertheless have the bags packed beforehand and the nursery all set for its occupant. Paul used this very image (v. 3) to describe the Day of the Lord, when Jesus will return to claim his own and establish his kingdom. We may be caught by surprise, but we must still be ready.

The consequences of being caught unprepared by a baby's insistence on being born are serious indeed. They pale, however, beside the eternal effects of not being ready when Jesus returns. We prepare ourselves just as Paul told us to (v. 8): We live in faith, hope, and love, ever on the alert for that great, promised day.

The call caught everyone in the stadium by surprise.
— Sportswriter Jeff Kanan on the fake field goal vs. Notre Dame

The timing of Jesus' return will be a surprise;
the consequences should not be.

FOOD FOR THOUGHT

Read Genesis 9:1-7.

"Everything that lives and moves will be food for you. Just as I gave you the green plants, I now give you everything" (v. 3).

In a sport with unforgiving weight requirements, MSU's only national champion wrestling team included "a gangle-armed farmer who hated to diet."

In 1967, the Spartans forced their way into the most exclusive club in college sports. Since 1928, Oklahoma State, Iowa State, and Oklahoma had won all but four of college wrestling's national titles. And then the Spartans won the 1967 title so convincingly they had it wrapped up before the final day's competition.

The head coach was Grady Peninger (1963-86), an MSU legend. He is a member of the Michigan State Athletics Hall of Fame and the U.S. Wrestling Hall of Fame.

The team was led by two-time Big-Ten champions Don Behm and Dale Anderson and a 167-pounder named George Radman, whom Peninger called "the cleverest wrestler I've ever coached." He was also the most vexing.

Radman was once described as "a beautifully proportioned young man with long, powerful arms" who "never felt in a hurry to go anywhere." That included making his weight before a match. He saw "no reason to suffer for a full week to make his weight limit when the same end [could] be achieved with a spine-rattling climax." "Once he was 11 pounds overweight the day before a meet," Peninger moaned.

On the day the '67 NCAAs began, Radman was a pound over the limit with 35 minutes to go. A frantic Peninger "rushed him into his sweat clothes and then into the steam room, where Radman ran in place and did push-ups until, with 90 seconds to go, he finally made weight."

Belly up to the buffet, boys and girls, for salad, dessert, sirloin steak, and prime rib. Rachael Ray's a household name; hamburger joints, pizza parlors, and taco stands lurk on every corner; and we have a TV channel devoted exclusively to food. We love our chow.

Food is one of God's really good ideas, but consider the complex divine plan that begins with a kernel and winds up with corn-on-the-cob slathered with butter and littered with salt. The creator of all life devised a downright fascinating and effective system in which living things are sustained and nourished physically through the sacrifice of other living things in a way similar to what Christ underwent to save us spiritually.

Whether it's fast food or home-cooked, practically everything we eat is a gift from God secured through a divine plan in which some plants and/or animals have given up their lives. Pausing to give thanks before we dive in seems the least we can do.

There wasn't one week George [Radman] didn't practically drive me out of my mind worrying about his weight.
— MSU wrestling head coach Grady Peninger

**God created a system that nourishes us
through the sacrifice of other living things;
that's worth a thank-you.**

FOOD FOR THOUGHT   87

FACING THE MUSIC

Read Psalm 98.

"Sing to the Lord a new song, for he has done marvelous things" (v. 1).

They're downright rowdy, they sit together at a Michigan State football game, and they dress funny. They are the 300 members of the Spartan Marching Band.

The MSU band is one of the oldest such units in the country. In 1870, Ransom McDonough Brooks created a ten-member student brass band and led them in parades and at drills. The original members, including Brooks, were all Civil War veterans.

In 1885, a permanent military department was established at what was then Michigan Agricultural College. The band thus became a Cadet Corps unit and appeared for the first time in uniform. They were gray with black braid trim. In those early days, the band performed at military drills and at public concerts.

For most of its existence, the band wore military khaki uniforms. That ended in 1952 when Michigan State began playing a Big Ten schedule. For the first time, the band wore the familiar green and white uniforms. Most of the inherited strict military uniform codes are still adhered to with squad leaders holding rigid inspections before every performance.

One of the more interesting aspects of the band's appearance at football games is that no flutes, clarinets, oboes, or bassoons are used. The opinion has always been that these instruments

SPARTANS

are too difficult for the fans to hear in the large Big Ten stadiums. Music majors specializing in those instruments usually play alto or tenor saxophones in the marching band. Tiny E-flat cornets are used to play the "woodwind-like" parts.

The Spartan band is one of the nation's most decorated units. In 1988, it received the Louis Sudler Trophy, which recognizes college marching bands of particular achievement. In 1995, ABC Sports chose the band to record its theme music for college football. The band has also played for five U.S. presidents.

Maybe you can't play a lick or carry a tune in the proverbial bucket. Or perhaps you do know your way around a guitar or a keyboard and can sing "Victory for MSU" on karaoke night without closing the joint down.

Unless you're a professional musician, however, how well you play or sing really doesn't matter. What counts is that you have music in your heart and sometimes you have to turn it loose.

Worshipping God has always included music in some form. That boisterous and musical enthusiasm you exhibit when the Spartan Marching Band strikes up during a football game should be a part of the joy you have in your personal worship of God.

Take a moment to count the blessings in your life, all gifts from God. Then consider that God loves you, he always will, and he has arranged through Jesus for you to spend eternity with him. How can that song God put in your heart not burst forth?

Just like music, sports elevates us to new levels of achievement.
— Drummer Randy Castillo

You call it music; others may call it noise;
sent God's way, it's called praise.

SMART MOVE

Read 1 Kings 4:29-34; 11:1-6.

"[Solomon] was wiser than any other man. . . . As Solomon grew old, his wives turned his heart after other gods, and his heart was not fully devoted to the Lord his God" (vv. 4:31, 11:4).

We need you down here." With that simple statement, MSU head coach Mark Dantonio made a move that salvaged the Spartans' fading championship hopes.

The first twenty minutes of the 2013 Big Ten championship game belonged to the Spartans as they rolled to a 17-0 lead over second-ranked and undefeated Ohio State. Then the script flipped. The Buckeye offense suddenly became unstoppable.

When OSU scored for the fourth time in six possessions to lead 24-17, Dantonio had seen enough carnage for one night. With about four minutes left in the third quarter, he put out a call to the press box for defensive coordinator Pat Narduzzi, who typically stays up top until the last few minutes of a game. Dantonio told his top assistant he needed him "with the [defensive] unit, pronto."

With Narduzzi on hand to look his guys in the eyes and talk to them, the defense regained its footing. The offense managed a field goal, and then the defense stuffed Ohio State on third-and-4. When Connor Cook hit tight end Josiah Price with a 9-yard touchdown pass, State had regained the lead at 27-24.

The defense later found itself under pressure after OSU partially blocked a punt. On fourth-and-2 at the MSU 39, linebacker Denicos Allen made the stop short of the marker. Six plays later, Jeremy Langford ripped off a game-clinching touchdown run.

The proof of just how smart Dantonio's move was? OSU didn't score a point after Narducci came down; the Buckeyes managed only 25 rushing yards in the fourth quarter.

The Spartans won 34-24 and were Big Ten champions.

Our moves often aren't as smart as was Mark Dantonio's summons of Pat Narduzzi. You ever wrecked the car when you spilled hot coffee on your lap? Fallen out of a boat on a cold morning? Locked yourself out of the house?

Formal education notwithstanding, we all make some dumb moves sometimes because time spent in a classroom is not an accurate gauge of common sense. Folks impressed with their own smarts often grace us with erudite pronouncements that we intuitively recognize as flawed, unworkable, or simply wrong.

A good example is the observation that great intelligence and scholarship are inherently incompatible with a deep and abiding faith in God. That is, the more we know, the less we believe. Any incompatibility occurs, however, only because we begin to trust in our own wisdom rather than the wisdom of God. We forget, as Solomon did, that God is the ultimate source of all our knowledge and wisdom and that even our ability to learn is a gift from God.

Not smart at all.

I'm like 'Oh, man, it's getting real. We've gotta step up.'
— Linebacker Denicos Allen on seeing Pat Narduzzi on the sideline

Being truly smart means trusting in God's wisdom rather than only in our own knowledge.

DAY 46

LAUGH IT UP

Read Genesis 21:1-7.

"Sarah said, 'God has brought me laughter, and everyone who hears about this will laugh with me'" (v. 6).

Quick-witted and affable, MSU icon Duffy Daugherty, still the school's all-time winningest football coach, could always spread a little laughter around no matter how dire the circumstances.

Daugherty had so many jokes stored up that he often told his team a new one after practice. Not surprisingly, he was a favorite among the reporters and on the banquet circuit for his one-liners and his sidesplitting remarks.

Among Daugherty's most famous witticisms:

• "I like those goal-line stands of ours, but I wish they'd make them up around the 50-yard line where I can see them better."

• "Me!" when asked whom he was most happy to see back for the 1965 season.

• "Oh, well, we have to learn to play on a wet field anyway," after spilling his coffee on a playbook while talking to reporters.

• "I told [assistant coach] Bob Devaney, who sits on the bench with me, that I thought it would be a good idea if he wore a jacket with 'Head Coach' in large letters," after receiving a death threat.

• The players "were so high this week that we had to shake the trees around the field to get them down for practice," after the 47-14 crushing of Notre Dame in 1956.

• "Imagine that. Lady Godiva couldn't pull half that crowd.

SPARTANS

People just aren't interested in looking at white horses," on being told 100,101 people were at the 28-0 defeat of Michigan in 1961.

- "Football is not a contact sport. It's a collision sport. Dancing is a contact sport."
- "Remember, Duffy, we're with you win or tie," on the contents of a letter he received from a State alumnus.
- "Sherman Lewis is a great football player with just one weakness: He's a senior."

Witty folks such as Duffy Daugherty and comedians stand out because they find humor in the world, and it's often hard for us to do that. "Laughter is foolish," an acerbic Solomon wrote in Ecclesiastes 2:2, his angst overwhelming him because he couldn't find much if anything in his world to laugh at.

We know how he felt. When we take a good look around at this world we live in, can we really find much to laugh at? It seems everywhere we look we find not just godlessness but ongoing and pervasive tragedy and misery.

Well, we can recognize as Sarah did that in God's innumerable gifts lie irresistible laughter. The great gift of Jesus provides us with more than enough reason to laugh no matter our situation. Through God's grace in Jesus Christ, we can laugh at death, at Satan, at the very gates of hell, at the world's pain.

Because they are of this world, our tears will pass. Because it is of God, our laughter will remain — forever.

We've learned our lesson. We'll never recruit anyone that smart again.
— Duffy Daugherty after center Walt Forman graduated as a junior

Of the world, sorrow is temporary;
of God, laughter is forever.

DAY 47

STEALING THE SHOW

Read Luke 10:30-37.

"Which of these three do you think was a neighbor to the man who fell into the hands of robbers?" (v. 36)

With a notorious gang of hoodlums from Detroit on hand, a panicked Michigan State business manager was convinced the thugs planned to steal the gate receipts.

During the summer of 1925, assistant coach Tarz Taylor had a summer job in Detroit that led him to become acquainted with "some strange characters." In the fall, Taylor asked for and received eight tickets for the Colgate game to give to some friends.

The local police told business manager Lyman L. Frimodig (the only athlete in MSU history to earn ten varsity letters) that those "friends" were members of the Purple Gang, "a powerful, murderous, prohibition-era, liquor-smuggling mob of hoodlums." They suspected the hoodlums would hold up the gate while they were in town. Frimodig determined to get all that cash from ticket sales to the school's vault as soon as possible.

Sure enough, the gang came rolling up to the stadium "in two big black limousines, just like in a James Cagney movie." They showed their tickets — no guns — and went to their seats.

Meanwhile, at halftime, Frimodig stuffed the receipts into canvas bank bags, jumped into the side car of a police motorcycle, and took off across an open field toward the vault. On the way, the motorcycle got stuck in some mud, and Frimodig had to get

SPARTANS

out and push. When he arrived at the vault, he discovered he was one bag short. "So back they went a-flying to locate the missing money." They found it and locked the funds away.

Back in the stadium, the gang members comported themselves quite well. Only after the game did they shake everyone up by whipping out their pistols and taking some practice shots at the ducks on the Red Cedar River before piling into their limousines.

By the way, State beat Colgate 14-0 that day.

Rare is the person of faith who can't quote God's eighth commandment: You shall not steal. That's pretty direct, but implicit in that order is a divine recognition of the right to personal property. Something can't be stolen if it isn't owned.

Theft in America is pandemic. From the penny-ante shoplifters to those who pad their expense accounts to the wealthy who lie and cheat on their taxes to the swindlers with a pyramid scheme. The prevalent attitude — like the robbers in Jesus' parable of the Good Samaritan — is that I will take your stuff because I can.

That doesn't make it right, especially in God's eyes. In fact, the attitude toward possessions that the person of faith should have is exemplified by the Good Samaritan himself: What is mine is yours to share if you need it.

The truth is that what we call "our" money and "our" stuff is really God's. To use it in ways other than those God has ordained is nothing less than stealing from God. As a result, we may ultimately rob ourselves of our eternal salvation.

Our sales in those days were greatest on the day of the game at the gate.
— Lyman Frimodig, explaining his concern about a possible robbery

'You shall not steal.' God meant it.

DAY 48

KEEP ON TRUCKING

Read Mark 14:32-42.

"'Father,' he said, 'everything is possible for you. Take this cup from me. Yet not what I will, but what you will'" (v. 36).

Persistence eventually prevailed and landed Tom Izzo a job as a Michigan State assistant.

Izzo is a college basketball icon who in 2016 was inducted into the Naismith Memorial Basketball Hall of Fame. He took over the Michigan State men's team in 1995 and since then has presided over one of the most successful collegiate basketball programs in the country. His 2000 team won the national championship; seven teams have made it to the Final Four. With more than 540 victories, he is the school's all-time winningest coach.

Izzo began his coaching career in 1977 with a high-school boys' team. After one season, he returned to Northern Michigan, his alma mater, as an assistant coach.

He soon began looking for a way to move up. In East Lansing for the high school state championships, he looked up Spartan head coach Jud Heathcote. "The young assistant worked up his nerve" to ask Heathcote if he had an opening on his staff. The boss Spartan was polite, but his answer was a firm "no."

A year later, Izzo tried again. His approach and Heathcote's answer were the same, but a broken jaw rendered the moment memorable. "I could hardly understand him," Heathcote recalled.

The third time turned out to be the charm for the persistent young assistant coach. When Izzo approached him a year later, Heathcote offered him a $7,000-a-year graduate assistant job. Izzo took it on the spot. He shared a two-bedroom apartment with one of the team managers, Mark Hollis, who in 2008 was appointed MSU's Athletic Director. For office space, the assistants crowded into one small room they nicknamed the Dungeon Room. They arranged their desks so they could shout at one another.

It wasn't much in the way of money, facilities, or prestige, but a persistent Tom Izzo was on his way.

Life is tough; it inevitably beats us up and kicks us around some. But life has four quarters, and so here we are, still standing, still in the game. We know we can never win if we don't finish. We emerge as winners and champions only if we never give up, if we just see it through as the young Tom Izzo did.

Jesus has been in a similar situation. On that awful night in the Garden of Gethsemane, our Lord understood the nature of the suffering he was about to undergo, and he begged God to take it from him. In the end, though, he yielded to God's will and surrendered his own.

Even in the matter of persistence, Jesus is our example. As he did, we push doggedly and determinedly ahead following God's will for our lives no matter how hard it gets. We can do it because God is with us.

I figured with his perseverance, he deserved something.
— Jud Heathcote on hiring Tom Izzo

It's tough to keep going no matter what, but you have almighty God's power to pull you through.

WORK ETHIC

Read Matthew 9:35-38.

"Then he said to his disciples, 'The harvest is plentiful but the workers are few. Ask the Lord of the harvest, therefore, to send out workers into his harvest field'" (vv. 37-38).

Told by his position coach why he wasn't good enough to play quarterback in the Big Ten, Dan Enos went to work.

Enos was not a particularly heralded recruit out of high school, but head coach George Perles figured he would make a Big Ten player. Offensive coordinator Morris Watts, who worked with the quarterbacks, wasn't convinced.

After a freshman season behind Bobby McAllister, Enos was uncertain whether he should stay or transfer. So he asked Watts: "Can I play here?" "I'm not sure," the coach answered. "Physically, your arm strength isn't sufficient to play at the Big Ten level." He also called attention to a hitch in Enos' delivery. He pretty much said Enos had more going against him than for him.

That was enough to discourage most players, but not Enos. He established a routine to increase his arm strength by throwing two to three hundred passes a day into a net. Receivers Courtney Hawkins and James Bradley and tight end Duane Young often joined him to catch balls for a while until he wore them out.

Enos prepared himself mentally, too. When he wasn't throwing, he was watching film. In team meetings, "he was insatiable when it came to information and strategy." He asked so many questions

Watts ruefully wondered if he wouldn't have more fun being a line coach.

All that work paid off. Enos was the starting quarterback in 1989 and 1990. He didn't have the howitzer for an arm coaches prefer, but he compensated for it with his leadership skills and the precision with which he ran the offense. He finished up with the third best career completion percentage (.621) in State history.

With a hard working Dan Amos at the helm, the Spartans went 16-7-1 with bowl wins over Hawaii and Southen Cal.

Do you embrace hard work or try to avoid it? No matter how hard you may try, you really can't escape hard work. Funny thing about all these labor-saving devices like cell phones and laptop computers: You're working longer and harder than ever. For many of us, our work defines us perhaps more than any other aspect of our lives. But there's a workforce you're a part of that doesn't show up in any Labor Department statistics or any IRS records.

You're part of God's staff; God has a specific job that only you can do for him. It's often referred to as a "calling," but it amounts to your serving God where there is a need in the way that best suits your God-given abilities and talents.

You should stand ready to work for God all the time, 24-7. Those are awful hours, but the benefits are out of this world.

Here was a kid whose work ethic was slowly turning him into a starting quarterback.
— Sportswriter Lynn Henning on Dan Enos

God calls you to work for him using the talents
and gifts he gave you; whether you're a worker
or a malingerer is up to you.

THE SUB

Read Galatians 3:10-14.

"Christ redeemed us from the curse of the law by becoming a curse for us" (v. 13).

The last thing the Spartans needed was to have their star middle linebacker suspended for what was arguably the program's biggest game in a generation. Good thing they had a sub.

As the Big-Ten champions prepared for their Rose-Bowl game against Stanford on Jan. 1, 2014, they received the unsettling news that their All-Big Ten linebacker would not play. Defensive coordinator Pat Narduzzi turned to senior Kyler Elsworth, who would be playing his last college game and making his first career start.

State had offered Elsworth a wrestling scholarship, but he had decided to pursue football instead. He walked on in East Lansing and earned a scholarship after two seasons.

So here he was, this career backup, taking the field on one of college football's biggest stages in the Spartans' first Rose Bowl appearance since 1988. Elsworth more than held his own as part of the stingiest defense in the country (248 yards allowed per game), making four tackles including 1.5 tackles for loss.

That last tackle propelled Elsworth into MSU football lore.

Behind Connor Cooks' career-high 332 passing yards and two touchdowns, State led 24-20 with under two minutes to play. The Cardinal had one last chance to save itself with a fourth-and-1 at its own 34. "The most physical team on the West Coast" lined up to power its way to the first down.

It ran into Elsworth instead. "Once I saw their offensive linemen's stance, I knew the way to make a play was for me to go over the top," Elsworth said. He did just that, vaulting into the air and colliding with the Stanford running back for no gain.

This career sub was named the game's defensive MVP for his play that sealed the Spartans' win.

Wouldn't it be cool if you had a substitute like Kyler Elsworth for all of life's hard stuff? Telling of a death in the family? Call in your sub. Ending a relationship? Big job interview? Crucial presentation at work? Let the sub handle it.

We do have such a substitute, but not just for the matters of life. Instead, Jesus is our substitute for matters of life and death. Since Jesus has already made it, we don't have to make the sacrifice God demands for forgiveness and salvation.

One of the more pathetic aspects of our contemporary times is that many people deny Jesus Christ and then desperately cast about for a substitute for him. Mysticism, human philosophies such as Scientology, false religions such as Hinduism and Islam, cults, New Age approaches that preach self-fulfillment without responsibility or accountability — they and others like them are all pitiful, inadequate substitutes for Jesus.

There is no substitute for Jesus. It's Jesus or nothing.

[Kyler] Elsworth [was] the unlikeliest of heroes as a fill-in for an accomplished defense.
— *Sportswriter Stephen Brooks in* Reaching Higher

**There is no substitute for Jesus,
the consummate substitute.**

DAY 51

HAVE COURAGE

Read 1 Corinthians 16:13-14.

"Be on your guard; stand firm in the faith; be men of courage; be strong" (v. 13).

Arthur Ray was so courageous he received an award for it.

Ray was a prize catch for State's 2008 recruiting class, the 18th-rated guard in the country. During his senior year of high school, however, he was diagnosed with cancer in his left leg and was told he would be lucky to ever walk again, let alone play football.

What followed was a litany of medical horror. Ray endured nine surgeries, including four bone grafts; he underwent chemotherapy and battled several outbreaks of infection. For almost two years, he couldn't walk without crutches.

All the while, Ray never gave up on his dream to play football for the Spartans. He postponed his enrollment at State for a year, and Mark Dantonio and his staff honored his scholarship.

He drew on a reservoir of courage he found in those around him who shared his suffering. "I'm walking through the hallways and there are kids in there — 7 and 8, 10, and 11 — brain tumors, stage four lymphoma, leukemia," Ray said. He recalled sitting in a common room with tiny chairs watching State play Wisconsin. "Yeah, Art! That's gonna be you!" the kids said. "I have a bald head, no eyebrows and the chemo is beating me up and I'm like, 'Y'all are right,'" Ray said. "I'm gonna get back."

He did. Doctors cleared Ray to practice in the spring of 2011.

SPARTANS

During a team meeting before the season opener, senior left guard and team captain Joel Foreman gave up his spot so Ray could start against Youngstown State. "It was symbolic — one snap, a short pass with slide protection," but Arthur Ray was on the field.

He saw spot duty in three other games for the Spartans in 2011. In December, the Football Writers Association of America awarded him its Courage Award. Ray went on to be a two-time captain for Fort Lewis College, a Division II school.

When we speak of courage, we often think of heroic actions such as that displayed by soldiers during wartime or firefighters during an inferno. But as Arthur Ray's successful battle to return to the football field shows, there is another aspect to courage.

What made Ray's fight against cancer courageous was not the absence of fear, which usually results from foolhardiness or a dearth of relevant information. Rather, his courage showed itself in his refusal to let fear, obstacles, and hardship debilitate him.

This is the courage God calls upon us to demonstrate in our faith lives. When Paul urged the Christians in Corinth to "be men of courage," he wasn't telling them to rush into burning buildings. He was admonishing them to be strong and sure in their faith.

This courageous attitude is an absolute necessity for American Christians today when our faith is under attack as never before. Our spiritual courage reveals itself in our proclaiming the name of Jesus no matter what forces are arrayed against us.

I couldn't have a bad day. Those kids meant too much to me.
— Arthur Ray on a source for his courage

To be courageous for Jesus is to speak his name boldly no matter what Satan may use against us.

DAY 52

ALIVE AGAIN

Read Matthew 28:1-10.

"He is not here; he has risen, just as he said. Come and see the place where he lay" (v. 6).

One writer called it the night Earvin Johnson came "back from the 'dead.'" So did the Michigan State season.

When the Spartans hosted Ohio State on Feb 1, 1979, a season of unprecedented promise was in real danger of slipping away. At the time, the Buckeyes were 8-0 in conference play while MSU's Big Ten record was 4-4. Another loss ended all hopes of a league title and probably finished off NCAA Tournament dreams also.

So Jenison Field House held its collective breath in dread late in the first half when Johnson "hit the floor writhing in pain" with an ankle injury. Team physician Dr. David Hough led a gimpy Johnson to the locker room. "We put [the ankle] on ice and watched it for a period of time," said trainer Clint Thompson.

Meanwhile, the 32-23 lead MSU had when Johnson went down disappeared. Ohio State took its first lead at 39-38 with 14:10 left to play. It didn't look good for the game or the season, since Johnson was obviously through for the night.

Well, maybe not. Johnson flatly told the doctor and the trainer he was going back in. So they taped him up for a trial run. "Earvin did enough for us to give him the okay," Thompson said.

Jay Vincent was at the free throw line with a 44-43 lead "when Earvin 'magically' reappeared." The place went totally bonkers.

SPARTANS

"It was absolutely the loudest I'd ever heard Jenison," Johnson said

Head coach Jud Heathcote said he waited one-third of a second after getting the word from Thompson that Johnson was good to go. With 8:42 left, Johnson was back on the court.

The Spartans beat Ohio State 84-79 in overtime and proceeded to rip off nine more wins in a row on the way to the Big Ten and the national titles. The run to glory and legend started that night Magic Johnson and the whole season came back from the dead.

All this language of resurrection is figurative, of course; neither Magic Johnson nor the team was literally dead. We often speak figuratively of resurrected careers in sports. We use resurrection language when a team comes from way behind to win a game.

While literal resurrections occur in the New Testament, one in particular stands alone. All except that one actually amount to resuscitations, the postponement of death. When Jesus walked out of that tomb on the first Easter morning, though, he threw off not only his burial cloths but death itself. On that day, God created something new: the resurrection life that come one glorious day will be the only one.

That's because the most shocking promise Jesus delivered from God to his children is that resurrection is a fact of life for his followers. When Christ left that tomb behind, he also left death behind for all who believe that he is indeed the savior of the world.

They'd already made up their mind that I wasn't going to play. I told them there's no holding me back; if we lost, there was no tomorrow.
— Magic Johnson on his 'resurrection' vs. Ohio State

Jesus' resurrection forever ended
death's hold on life; life has won.

DAY 53

CALLING IT QUITS

Read Numbers 13:25-14:4.

"The men who had gone up with him said, 'We can't attack those people; they are stronger than we are'" (v. 13:31).

Josiah Price seriously thought about quitting football at Michigan State. But then there was Barak.

Price finished his career in East Lansing in 2016 with 21 touchdown catches, the most in school history by a tight end.

He grew up in Greentown, Ind., a small rural town with six churches and one stoplight. When he began to excel in football in high school, he considered transferring to a private school in Indianapolis to get noticed by recruiters. His mom put an end to that. "If God wants you to play football somewhere else," she said, "then He can find you here in Greentown."

Mark Dantonio found him there. Price arrived on campus in the fall of 2012; it didn't go well. For the first time in his life, football was hard. He was no longer the strongest or the fastest, and extra hours of practice and work didn't seem to close the gap.

School was hard, too. The small-town boy had trouble adjusting to city life and the sheer size of everything from the 50,000-student campus to the massive football stadium.

So, Price thought long and hard about quitting, about heading back home and taking a job at his dad's auto dealership. Without really doing so, Barak talked him out of it.

SPARTANS

Barak is Josiah's younger brother by nine years. He has cerebral palsy, but that has not been able to temper his indomitable spirit. Josiah saw the happiness his brother experienced from his being a Spartan. Prior to every game, the brothers shared a hug before Josiah left to put on his pads. Barak went to every away game and was always waiting when the team bus pulled in. Many of the players shared a fist-bump with their adopted teammate with the dynamic personality who wore green-and-white hearing aids.

Josiah just couldn't take that away from his brother. He stayed.

Did you ever quit a high-school sports team because you knew you weren't going to get to play? Bail out of a relationship that was obviously going nowhere? Walk away from a job that didn't offer much of a future? Quitting may be painful, but sometimes it's the most sensible way to minimize your losses. At times, you may well give up on something or someone.

In your relationship with God, however, you should remember the people of Israel, who quit when the Promised Land was theirs for the taking. They forgot one fact of life you never should: God never gives up on you.

That means you should never, ever give up on God. No matter how tired or discouraged you get, no matter that it seems your prayers aren't getting through to God, no matter what — quitting on God is not an option. He is preparing a blessing for you, and in his time, he will bring it to fruition — if you don't quit on him.

Once you learn to quit, it becomes a habit.

— *Vince Lombardi*

Whatever else you give up on in your life, don't give up on God; he will never ever give up on you.

UNEXPECTEDLY

Read Matthew 24:36-51.

"No one knows about that day or hour, not even the angels in heaven, nor the Son, but only the Father" (v. 36).

No one could possibly have expected who the hero would be in an MSU upset of Ohio State. That's because his name wasn't even in the game program.

A couple of weeks into the 1972 season, "a slender young man with shoulder-length hair" walked up to head coach Duffy Daugherty at practice and introduced himself. He was Dirk Krijt, a foreign student from The Netherlands. He had never seen a football game and had no clue what a touchdown was. He told Daugherty, however, that he had played soccer and wanted to see if he could kick a football.

Lacking a good kicker, the head Spartan figured he had nothing to lose. The staff rounded up a sweat suit and some soccer-style shoes, hauled a sack of footballs to one end of the field, and turned Krijt loose. As Daugherty put it, "He could kick, all right."

The head coach assigned Krijt to the junior varsity, but then the week of the Ohio State game, Daugherty elevated him to the varsity. Thus, his name wasn't in the game program.

This totally unexpected hero kicked four field goals as MSU upset the 5th-ranked Buckeyes 19-12. (See Devotion No. 95.)

The media flooded into the State locker room after the game. To Daugherty's consternation, Krijt strolled by smoking a cigarette.

SPARTANS

He then announced he was celebrating that night with a girl and a few beers and invited a flustered Daugherty to join him.

When one of the reporters inquired about the training rules at State and how they related to cigarettes, booze, and women, Daugherty was ready with his answer. "We have a new rule," he said. "Anyone who can kick four field goals in one game is allowed to do most anything he likes."

Just like the favored Buckeyes, we think we've got everything figured out and under control, and then something unexpected like Dirk Krijt happens. About the only thing we can expect from life with any certainty is the unexpected.

God is that way too, suddenly showing up to remind us he's still around. A friend who calls and tells you he's praying for you, a hug from your child or grandchild, a lone lily that blooms in your yard — unexpected moments when the divine comes crashing into our lives with such clarity that it takes our breath away and brings tears to our eyes.

But why shouldn't God do the unexpected? The only factor limiting what God can do in our lives is the paucity of our own faith. We should expect the unexpected from God, this same deity who caught everyone by surprise by unexpectedly coming to live among us as a man, and who will return when we least expect it.

Sports is about adapting to the unexpected and being able to modify plans at the last minute.
        — Sir Roger Bannister, first-ever sub-four-minute miler

**God continually does the unexpected,
like showing up as Jesus,
who will return unexpectedly.**

DAY 55

THE GREATEST

Read Mark 9:33-37.

"If anyone wants to be first, he must be the very last, and the servant of all" (v. 35).

The greatest rushing performance in NCAA history to that time wasn't going to happen — until the guys in the press box let the State coaches know what was going on.

As a senior in 1971, running back and team co-captain Eric Allen was a first-team All-American and the Big Ten MVP. He set nine school records as he led the league in rushing, rushing touchdowns, and scoring. He became the first player in Big Ten history to score more than one hundred points in a season.

The highlight of Allen's season came in a 43-10 beatdown of Purdue on Oct. 30. He romped for 189 yards rushing in the first half and had touchdown runs of 24 and 59 yards. That outburst sent Spartan sports information gurus to the record books. They found that both the NCAA and the Big Ten single-game rushing record was 347 yards, still far out of Allen's reach.

But early in the third quarter, Allen accounted for 59 yards on a Spartan touchdown drive. Now the staffers became excited and started keeping a running total. Allen kept running until early in the fourth quarter, he had 325 yards. Then "to the consternation of the frantically calculating Spartan sports information people," Allen trotted to the sideline. He was done for the day.

But the press box guys asked the Spartan coaches working the press box phones to relay to the bench the word that Allen was just 23 yards shy of the all-time NCAA single-game rushing record. Offensive line coach Gordie Serr took the message, nodded, and said something to head coach Duffy Daugherty.

Daugherty threw an arm around Allen's shoulder and said, "You're going back [in] and are going to carry the ball on every play until you get [the record." Allen did, capping off the greatest game in NCAA rushing history with 350 yards and an NCAA-record 397 all-purpose yards.

We all want to be the greatest. The goal for the Spartans and their fans every season is the national championship. The competition at work is to be the most productive sales person on the staff or the Teacher of the Year. In other words, we define being the greatest in terms of the struggle for personal success. It's nothing new; Jesus' disciples saw greatness in the same way.

As Jesus illustrated, though, greatness in the Kingdom of God has nothing to do with the secular world's understanding of success Rather, the greatest are those who channel their ambition toward the furtherance of Christ's kingdom through love and service, rather than their own advancement. This is, obviously, a complete reversal of status and values as the world sees them.

But who could be greater than the person who has Jesus for a brother and God for a father? And that's every one of us.

Not Red Grange nor O.J. Simpson ever had a better game than [Allen's].
— State SID Fred W. Stabley on the '71 Purdue game

**To be great for God has nothing to do
with personal advancement and everything to do
with the advancement of Christ's kingdom.**

BONE TIRED

Read Matthew 11:27-30.

"Come to me, all you who are weary and burdened, and I will give you rest" (v. 28).

For most of her first two years at MSU, Kristin Haynie was tired. The problem and the solution for it — well, if they weren't true, they'd be unbelievable.

Haynie was a senior point guard for the greatest team in Spartan women's basketball history. That would be the 2004-05 squad that set a school record with 33 wins and advanced to the finals of the NCAA Tournament. An honorable mention All-America, Haynie set a State season record with 117 steals. She finished up as the fourth player in Big Ten history to accumulate career totals of 1,000 points, 500 rebounds, 500 assists and 300 steals. She set State career records with 574 assists and 346 steals

It was obvious, though, that something was dreadfully wrong during Haynie's freshman and sophomore seasons. "I used to get really tired all the time," she recalled.

Doctors were confounded that an apparently perfectly healthy young woman spent most of her time abnormally tired. Blood tests and other examinations yielded no clues. Then "almost as an afterthought," somebody — name unknown — happened to mention to Haynie's doctors that out of concern for cancer, her large intestine had been removed when she was 11! Thus, her body couldn't absorb most nutrients.

SPARTANS

The solution was a diet that "would put most people under the care of a cardiologist." Between meals, Haynie consumed thick shakes that contributed to a daily intake of at least 4,000 calories, almost twice that required by a typical active young person.

The diet turned Haynie's life and the team's fortunes around. She became what Spartan forward Kelli Roehrig called "a little fireball." With newfound energy, ebullience replaced her previously natural shyness, and she became a team leader.

The everyday struggles and burdens of life beat us down. They may be enormous; they may be trivial with a cumulative effect. But they tire us out.

Doctors don't help too much. Sleeping pills can zonk us out; muscle relaxers can dull the weariness. Other than that, it's drag on as usual until we can collapse exhaustedly into bed.

Then along comes Jesus, as usual offering hope and relief for what ails us, though in a totally unexpected way. He says take my yoke. Whoa, there! Isn't a yoke a device for work? Exactly.

The mistake we all too often make lies in trying to do it alone. We rely on ourselves instead of Jesus. If we yoke ourselves to our Lord, the unimaginable, limitless power of almighty God is at our disposal to do the heavy lifting for us.

God's strong shoulders and broad back can handle any burdens we can give him. We just have to let them go.

My sophomore year I was drained all the time.
    — Kristin Haynie on the fatigue that once dominated her life

Tired and weary are a way of life
only when we fail to accept Jesus' invitation
to swap our burden for his.

DAY 57

THE INTERVIEW

Read Romans 14:1-12.

*"We will all stand before God's judgment seat. . . . So
then, each of us will give an account of himself to God"
(vv. 10, 12).*

Nick Saban wasn't really a serious candidate to become Michigan State's head football coach — until he had an interview.

After twelve seasons and 73 wins, George Perles was fired in November 1994. He left in his wake a college president, Peter McPherson, who "had no intention of hiring a coach who had been any part of the Perles regime." That included Saban, who had been on Perles' staff from 1983-87.

Nevertheless, Saban's resume and his love for MSU were just too good for the search committee members to ignore. He made it onto the short list of persons to be interviewed, especially after impressing McPherson with a highly personal letter in which he explained why he wanted to be State's head coach.

The interviews of the prospective coaches on the short list left committee members unimpressed. One was so bad the coach's chances were dead in less than an hour. Another said he would keep all the current assistants. Bad move.

And then there was Saban. He showed up more prepared than any of the other candidates. He laid out a vision for State football that included a prepared list of the assistants he would try to hire. He talked about academics, integrity, and discipline, about inspiration and motivation. "He covered every topic the committee had outlined. And he never slipped up." During the session conducted over a meal, he was so absorbed that he never touched his silverware or his club sandwich.

The virtuoso performance turned sentiment Saban's way. After a brief, unsatisfactory flirtation with a Penn State assistant, the school president put aside his reservations about Perles' assistant coaches. On Saturday, Dec. 16, Nick Saban was introduced at a news conference as MSU's twentieth head football coach.

You know all about job interviews. You've experienced the stress, the anxiety, the helpless feeling that's part of any interview. You tried to appear calm and relaxed while struggling to come up with reasonably original answers to banal questions.

We all will undergo one final interview on God's great Judgment Day when we must give an accounting of ourselves. John 5:22-23 declares that God has committed all judgment to Jesus, a rather startling example of one of the New Testament's consistent themes: that the Father and the Son are one.

In our final interview, Jesus will judge each of us according to the rules laid out by God the Father. All eternity will be at stake and a resume of good deeds, sterling accomplishments, and unblemished grade-point averages won't help. The only way to ace this one is to have Jesus know who you are through your faith in him.

Saban flew back to Cleveland knowing he had nailed the interview.
— *Sportswriter Lynn Henning in* Spartan Seasons II

In our final interview, Jesus will judge us using God's criteria, including faith in the Son.

DAY 58

GOOD ADVICE

Read Isaiah 9:2-7.

"And he will be called Wonderful Counselor" (v. 9:6b).

Frustrated and disappointed, Tony Lippett's football career at MSU turned around with the advice he got from one phone call.

In September of 2013, Lippett was a junior wide receiver who hadn't started any of the first four games and had caught only four passes. He called his former mentor and high school coach, Rod Oden, to vent his frustration. "I haven't done anything wrong," he complained. "Why am I not playing? I'm at the point where I don't even need to shower after games."

Fortunately for Lippett and the Spartans, Oden offered some encouragement and some good advice for the youngster he considered one of the most dynamic players he had ever coached. He told me "I could go out and play this game at a high level, if I had the heart and desire," Lippett recalled. Then Oden advised the anxious junior to go build a bridge with his position coach, Terrence Samuel. "Do the things they wanted to see out of [him] day in and day out," Oden said.

An introvert by nature, Lippett followed Oden's advice though it meant an uncharacteristically aggressive move for him. He went to Samuel, and they talked and ate breakfast together. The coach had some advice of his own. He suggested Lippett watch some films of MSU greats like Plaxico Burress and Charles Rogers; then he should look at some film of himself. Lippett had little trouble seeing the difference.

He went to work with Samuel, followed his advice, and transformed himself. He led the team in receptions that season; then as a senior in 2014, he was the Big Ten Receiver of the Year and first-team All-Big Ten. He was drafted by the Miami Dolphins.

As Tony Lippett did, we all need a little advice now and then. More often than not, we turn to professional counselors, who are all over the place. Marriage counselors, grief counselors, guidance counselors in our schools, rehabilitation counselors, all sorts of mental health and addiction counselors: We can find plenty of advice for the taking.

The problem, of course, is that we find advice easy to offer but hard to take. We also have a rueful tendency to solicit the wrong source for advice, seeking counsel that doesn't really solve our problem but that instead enables us to continue with it.

Our need for outside advice, for an independent perspective on our situation, is actually God-given. God serves many functions in our lives, but one role clearly delineated in his Word is that of Counselor. Jesus himself is described as the "Wonderful Counselor." All the advice we need in our lives is right there for the asking; we don't even have to pay for it except with our faith. God is always there for us: to listen, to lead, and to guide.

[The advice] forced me to look in the mirror and stop looking at everybody else.
— *Tony Lippett on turning his career around*

**We all need and seek advice in our lives,
but the ultimate and most wonderful Counselor
is of divine and not human origin.**

DAY 59

CHANGING TIMES

Read Romans 6:1-14.

*"Just as Christ was raised from the dead through the glory
of the Father, we too may live a new life" (v. 4).*

The country was changing, and Michigan State harnessed those changes for unprecedented success on the football field.

Led by head coach Duffy Daugherty, MSU won national championships in 1965 and 1966 "with some of the most racially and geographically integrated teams in all of college football." That roster wasn't accidental, but intentional.

In the early 1960s, Daugherty turned an appraising look at the Deep South. What he saw was a whole bunch of outstanding football players who couldn't play at major Southern schools because of segregation. So he acted. "If they could have played down South, they would have probably stayed down there," said Hank Bullough, a Daugherty assistant from 1959-69. "But they couldn't. So we hit the South. It was a new place to go."

Many of the coaching icons of the South such as Bear Bryant at Alabama and Frank Howard at Clemson helped Daugherty's recruiting efforts. They would call Daugherty if they ran across a player they knew could play in the Big Ten. The result was a 1965 roster that included 18 black players, nine from the South. The '66 roster featured 17 black players, 10 from the South.

The first real push came in 1963 when State brought in players such as Bubba Smith, Gene Washington, George Webster, Charles

SPARTANS

Thornhill, Ernie Pasteur, and Clinton Jones. One of the greatest classes in college football history, it included three future Hall of Famers and four of the top eight picks in the 1967 NFL draft.

The move from the South to MSU was quite a change for the players, too. For the first time, as quarterback Jimmy Raye put it, they found "an atmosphere of acceptance." Washington had never played with or against white players, and he found himself rooming with two white swimmers from Indiana.

Duffy Daugherty paid attention to the changes taking place in American culture and used them to his advantage. In our individual lives, we must be aware of the need for change. Every life has doubt, worry, fear, failure, frustration, unsuccessful relationships, and unfulfilled dreams in some combination. The memory and consequences of our past often haunt and trouble us.

Simply recognizing the need for change in our lives, though, doesn't mean the changes that will bring about hope, joy, peace, and fulfillment will occur. We need some power greater than ourselves or we wouldn't be where we are.

So where can we turn to? Where lies the hope for a changed life? It lies in an encounter with the Lord of all Hope: Jesus Christ. For a life turned over to Jesus, change is inevitable. With Jesus in charge, the old self with its painful and destructive ways of thinking, feeling, loving, and living is transformed.

A changed life is always only a talk with Jesus away.

Everything was completely segregated in Texas. All of a sudden, I'm in a friendly atmosphere. It was just a great, great welcoming.
— Gene Washington on the changed world he found at MSU

In Jesus lie the hope and the power to change lives.

MAMA'S BOY

Read John 19:25-30.

"Near the cross of Jesus stood his mother" (v. 25).

Mary Babers did something to her son so horrible the school athletic director said she was ruining his life. Instead, she saved it.

Babers' son is Draymond "Day-Day" Green, one of Michigan State's greatest basketball players ever and an NBA All-Star. As a senior at MSU in 2012, he was a first-team All-America, the Big Ten Player of the year, and the coaches' national player of the year.

Basketball was always the focus of his life. "It was basketball one through four, then school five and then basketball six through ten," he said when he was in the ninth grade. Those priorities resulted in a lackadaisical attitude toward schoolwork.

One phone call shattered his happy-go-lucky world. Shortly before the end of Green's ninth-grade school year, his science teacher called his mother to tell her he had cheated on a test. Her reaction was fury of the highest order, mostly at her son's laziness. Her punishment was immediate — and ultimately unimaginable by everyone else.

First, she took away all his electronics, including TV, for the summer. Then she hauled his bed out of his bedroom. And then Babers "went for the jugular." She took away basketball for the summer. That meant no AAU play with its national exposure so crucial for a player with the talent to play college ball.

Babers found no support for what she was doing. The school's athletic director called to plead her son's case. Her own parents said she'd gone too far. Green, of course, cried and begged for pity practically every day — especially when she made him walk to summer classes. When she was alone, Babers shed her own tears.

But she remained steadfast. "What I'm talking about is life," she said. "I am not going to fail him, and he is not going to fail."

A child grew up that summer. Green never had a GPA less than 3.2 again. Years later, he said, "If my mom didn't do what she did, I wouldn't be [at Michigan State]. I wouldn't have had the grades."

Mamas often do the sort of thing Mary Babers did for Draymond Green: do the best thing for her child even when it hurts her. No mother in history, though, has faced a challenge to match that of Mary, whom God chose to be the mother of Jesus. Like mamas and their children throughout time, Mary experienced both joy and perplexity in her relationship with her son.

To the end, though, Mary stood by her boy. She followed him all the way to his execution, an act of love and bravery since Jesus was condemned as an enemy of the Roman Empire.

But just as mothers like Mary Babers and Jesus' mother, Mary, would apparently do most anything for their children, so will God do anything out of love for his children. After all, that was God on the cross at the foot of which Mary stood, and he was dying for you, one of his children.

On his own, [Draymond Green] wrote a letter to his mother, apologizing for what he did and thanking her for what she'd done for him.
— ESPN's Dana O'Neil on the summer of Green's punishment

Like mothers, God will do anything out of love for his children; that includes dying on a cross.

DAY 61

MIRACLE PLAY

Read Matthew 12:38-42.

"He answered, 'A wicked and adulterous generation asks for a miraculous sign!'" (v. 39)

Chester Brewer wrought an athletic miracle."

So declared former Michigan State Sports Information Director Fred W. Stabley in his book *The Spartans*. Brewer's miracle was what he did with the football program at what was then Michigan Agricultural College. "In 1903, he took over a bumbling Michigan Aggie football program" that had won only nineteen games in its first seven seasons "and immediately revolutionized it." His first team went 6-1-1, by far the program's best season ever. In his eight falls as MAC's head coach, Brewer "put together the fantastic record for the tiny farmer's college" of 54-10-6.

Brewer never had a losing season. The 1908 squad went undefeated with two ties; three other teams lost only one game. That was miraculous enough for a program that had never before won more than four games in a season. But Brewer's leadership and success stabilized football at MAC when its existence was in doubt. He "completely won over a recalcitrant faculty. . . . [S]tudent support reached all-time highs. Financial problems abated."

And Brewer didn't roll up the wins against cupcakes. He made a determined effort to move MAC into big-time football by upgrading the schedule. The first big accomplishment was a 0-0 tie with Michigan in 1908. Players were carried from the field to the locker room. Some 600 students took to the streets and snake-danced through Lansing in celebration.

In 1910, the "Fighting Farmers" crushed Notre Dame 17-0, ruining an undefeated season for the Irish, and beat Marquette 3-2. "Brewer was simply the biggest thing that had ever happened to MAC," but he left after that 1910 season to coach at Missouri.

What Chester Brewer did at MAC may not classify as a true miracle reflecting divine intervention, but it did defy rational explanation and expectations as miracles do. How else can we explain escaping with only minor abrasions from an accident that totals the car? Or recovering from a so-called terminal illness?

Underlying the notion of miracles is the idea that they are rare instances of direct divine intervention that reveal God. But life shows us quite the contrary, that miracles are anything but rare. Since God made the world and everything in it, everything around you is miraculous. Even you are a miracle.

Your life thus can be mundane, dull, and ordinary, or it can be spent in a glorious attitude of childlike wonder and awe. It depends on whether you see the world through the eyes of faith. Only through faith can you discern the hand of God in any event; only through faith can you see the miraculous and thus see God.

Jesus knew that miracles don't produce faith, but rather faith produces miracles.

No man did more to persuade the faculty, the Board, and the older
alumni organized athletics could be compatible with higher education.
   — Former State SID Fred Stabley on Chester Brewer's miracle

Miracles are all around us,
but it takes the eyes of faith to see them.

HURRY UP AND WAIT

Read Acts 1:1-14.

"Do not leave Jerusalem, but wait for the gift my Father promised, which you have heard me speak about" (v. 4).

Keith Nichol stood patiently waiting to see where the ball would fall. He didn't know it, but he was about to complete one of the most iconic plays in Michigan State football history.

On Oct. 22, 2011, Wisconsin and Michigan State were tied at 31 with only four seconds left on the clock. The Spartans sat on the Badger 44, too far away for a field goal. Their only hope to avoid overtime lay in a desperate heave into the end zone.

State had a play ready, a "last-ditch, jump ball pass into the end zone." The offense had practiced it every Thursday just in case it was needed someday. Even head coach Mark Dantonio admitted, "That usually doesn't happen."

But they needed it now, and so they ran the Rocket.

Quarterback Kirk Cousins took the snap, stepped back, and heaved the ball long, high, and hard. Downfield, senior wide receiver B.J. Cunningham and sophomore tight end Dion Sims were already waiting. Nichol, a senior wide receiver, was there, too, but he had stopped a couple of yards short of the end zone. There he stood, waiting to see what happened.

The Wisconsin defense, of course, was ready, but the defender in the prime position to bat the ball away mistimed his leap. It bounced off Cunningham's face mask right back to Nichol inside the one-yard line. He was hit immediately, but as Cousins put it, "He used all of his strength to power into the end zone."

The officials initially ruled Nichol had been stopped short of the goal line. So began an interminable wait for a review that stretched on and on. Finally, the decision came and the wait was over: Nichol had broken the plane. Touchdown State. 37-31 win.

You rush to your doctor's appointment and wind up sitting in the appropriately named waiting room for an hour. You wait in the concessions line at an MSU game. You're put on hold when you call a tragically misnamed "customer service" center. All of that waiting is time in which we seem to do nothing but feel the precious minutes of our life ticking away.

Sometimes we even wait for God. We have needs, and in our desperation, we call upon the Lord. We are then disappointed if we don't get an immediate answer to our prayers.

But Jesus' last command to his disciples was to wait. Moreover, the entire of our Christian life is spent in an attitude of waiting for Jesus' return. While we wait for God, we hold steadfast to his promises, and we continue our ministry; we remain in communion with him through prayer and devotion.

In other words, we don't just wait; we grow stronger in our faith. Waiting for God is never time lost.

A Hail Mary with no time on the clock with the added bonus of a long review to keep everyone nervous for a bit longer is pretty dramatic.
— SpartanDan on the wait at the end of MSU-Wisconsin in 2011

Since God acts on his time and not ours,
we often must wait for him,
using the time to strengthen our faith.

STAR POWER

Read Luke 10:1-3, 17-20.

"The Lord appointed seventy-two others and sent them two by two ahead of him to every town and place where he was about to go" (v. 1).

Prior to the 2016 season, *ESPN*'s Brian Bennett admitted he was "scrambling for some actual football discussion" and offered his "All-21st-Century" team for Michigan State.

Let the debate begin with Bennett's list of the brightest Spartan stars who have played since 2000:

OFFENSE
- **Quarterback**: Connor Cook with "all the big wins, all the records"
- **Running Backs**: Le'Veon Bell and Javon Ringer
- **Wide Receivers**: B.J. Cunningham (who set school records for career receptions and receiving yards), Tony Lippett, Charles Rogers
- **Offensive Linemen**: Jack Conklin, Jack Allen, Joel Foreman, Sean Poole (who once earned Big Ten Player of the Week honors, a rarity for an offensive lineman), Shaun Mason

DEFENSE
- **Defensive Linemen**: Shilique Calhoun, Malik McDowell, Jerel Worthy, Marcus Rush
- **Linebackers**: Max Bullough, Greg Jones, Denicos Allen
- **Defensive Backs**: Darqueze Dennard, Trae Waynes, Kurtis

SPARTANS

Drummond, Johnny Adams

SPECIALISTS

- **Punter**: Brandon Fields, for whom the Big Ten's punter of the year award is named
- **Kicker**: Dan Conroy
- **Kick Returner**: DeAndra' Cobb

Football teams are like other organizations in that they may have stars such as the Spartans listed here, but the star would be nothing without the supporting cast. It's the same in a private company, in a government bureaucracy, in a military unit, and just about any other team of people with a common goal.

That includes the team known as a church. It may have its "star" in the preacher, who is — like the quarterback or the company CEO — the most visible representative of the team. Preachers are, after all, God's paid, trained professionals.

But when Jesus rounded up a team of seventy-two folks and sent them out, he didn't have any experienced evangelists or any educated seminary graduates on his payroll. All he had was a bunch of no-names who loved him. Centuries later, nothing has changed. God's church still depends on those whose only pay is the satisfaction of serving and whose only qualification is their abiding love for God. God's church needs you.

This is the top lineup Michigan State could field consisting of players who have played since 2000.
— Brian Bennett on his 'All-21st-Century' team

Yes, the church needs its professional clergy, but it also needs those who serve as volunteers because they love God; the church needs you.

UGLY AS SIN

Read Romans 7:14-25.

"I know that nothing good lives in me, that is, in my sinful nature. For I have the desire to do what is good, but I cannot carry it out" (v. 16).

To advance to the NCAA finals and win the 2000 national championship, the Spartans first had to win one ugly basketball game.

Junior guard Charlie Bell, who was named the team's Defensive Player of the Year in each of the four years he played, anticipated what kind of game the semifinal match against Wisconsin would be. "We can slow it down, get offensive rebounds and hurt people," he said.

The match-up in the semis was the fourth time the two Big Ten foes had clashed that season. State had taken the other three by scores of 61-44, 59-54, and 55-46. No fans or reporters in their right minds expected a run-and-gun game in the tourney semis.

They didn't get it. What they got, at least in the first half, was some really ugly basketball. Wisconsin went six minutes without scoring a basket, but Michigan State embarked on a drought of its own that at one stretch went almost twice that long. The Spartans "seemed to be dragging the game back into prehistory with them," declared *Sports Illustrated*'s Alexander Wolff.

When the clock ticked down to zero and mercifully ended the first half, State led 19-17. On the night before the game, former Spartans coach Jud Heathcote had asserted, "The first team to 40 will win." As Wolff put it, the coach "hadn't allowed for the possibility that neither team would crack that mark."

But both teams did. In the last half, State's star forward, Morris Peterson, the Big Ten Player of the Year, keyed a 13-2 Spartan run with ten points. That outburst effectively decided the outcome. Mo Pete finished with a game-high 20 points.

State won 53-41, which, as it turned out, wasn't ugly at all.

We live in a fallen world, a cursed one if you will. The glorious day when Jesus returns to set things right actually entails a return to what God's beautiful creation was before disobedience to God brought ugly into the world. All that disobedience can be encapsulated into one little three-letter word: sin.

"Ugly as sin" thus is not some routine and pointless cliché. Everything that is ugly in this world spawns from humanity's sin, from our insistence that we — and not God — know best. As Paul declares in the heartrending verses 7:21-24, evil in the form of sin is always right here with us. Even the best of us — including Paul — cannot stamp sin, willful or otherwise, out of our lives. The ugly is part of us; it comes with the territory. Sadly and horribly, the result is inevitably death.

In ourselves, we are irredeemably ugly and hopeless. In Christ, we are redeemably beautiful, and hope is our inheritance. Such is the power of salvation through our faith in Jesus.

Michigan State's fourth meeting with Wisconsin this season proved anew the adage, Familiarity breeds contemptible basketball.
— SI's Alexander Wolff on how ugly the game was

**In Christ, we no longer are ugly and hopeless in
our sin but beautiful and hopeful in our salvation.**

DAY 65

FAMILY TIES

Read Mark 3:31-35.

*"[Jesus] said, 'Here are my mother and my brothers!
Whoever does God's will is my brother and sister and
mother'" (vv. 34-35).*

When Riley Bullough led the Spartans in tackles in 2015, he was just doing what his family has done for generations.

The Bullough family has been dubbed the "First Family of Football" at Michigan State. It all started with Hank Bullough, who was a guard from 1952-54 and later coached at MSU.

Hank's sons, Shane and Chuck, both played linebacker at MSU. Shane led the team in tackles in 1985 and '86; Chuck was the leading tackler in 1990 and '91. Shane's oldest son Max, a third-team All-American linebacker in 2013, was the Spartans' leading tackler in 2011 and '12.

Thus, when Riley Bullough, son of Shane and brother of Max, had 106 tackles as a junior linebacker in 2015, it was the seventh time someone from the Bullough family had led the team in tackles. The "first family" tradition continued when Byron, the youngest of the three brothers and also a linebacker, earned a pair of letters in 2015 and '16.

The family's athletic ties to Michigan State deepened when the youngest Bullough sibling, Holly, joined the Spartans' track and cross-country teams as a freshman in 2016. Her uncle, Bobby Morse, has said she is probably the most competitive of the four.

SPARTANS

And in a house full of young athletes, there was always competition, so much so that at times the home looked like some sort of athletic compound. For instance, one morning before daylight and before school, a guard in the community where they lived was flabbergasted to discover the three boys playing basketball on a lighted court while Holly, a second-grader, jumped rope on the deck. "What are they doing over at that house?" he asked.

Just being the Bulloughs, a family for which faithful Michigan State fans will forever be grateful.

Some wit said families are like fudge, mostly sweet with a few nuts. You can probably call the names of your sweetest relatives, whom you cherish, and of the nutty ones too, whom you mostly try to avoid at a family reunion.

Like it or not, you have a family, and that's God's doing. God cherishes the family so much that he chose to live in one as a son, a brother, and a cousin.

One of Jesus' more radical actions was to redefine the family. No longer is it a single household of blood relatives or even a clan or a tribe. Jesus' family is the result not of an accident of birth but rather a conscious choice. All those who do God's will are members of Jesus' family.

What a startling and downright wonderful thought! You have family members out there you don't even know who stand ready to love you just because you're part of God's family.

As you can see, there is no shortage of athletes in this family.
— Writer Scott DeCamp on the generations of Bullough athletes

**For followers of Jesus, family comes not
from a shared ancestry but from a shared faith.**

PROVE IT!

Read John 2:18-25.

"Then the Jews demanded of him, 'What miraculous sign can you show us to prove your authority?'" (v. 18)

He was not seen as a big-time football player, so he had a lot to prove at Michigan State. He became a legend.

This lightly regarded player was termed "one of the least heralded members of MSU's 1975 recruiting class. An add-on. A dark horse. A guy who might be a decent special teams player some day." So all he did was become "one of Michigan State's most celebrated sports figures." He was Kirk Gibson.

At the time, college coaches really had only one useful tool at their disposal from which to glean information about recruits: game films. In the fall of 1974, assistant coach Andy MacDonald was in the midst of a late-night session with a projector in his office. He was scouting a target when an opponent's tailback caught his eye. He decided that player was worth a second look. It was Gibson, who was set, he thought, to play for Central Michigan in the Mid-American Conference because he had no other choice.

That second look led to a scholarship. Aware he had to prove himself, Gibson spent the summer of 1975 working to increase his speed. He arrived in the fall determined to compete. He did more than that. When fall camp ended, he was a starting receiver, outrunning and outhitting his teammates from day one.

In his second game, Gibson caught a 56-yard TD pass to beat

SPARTANS

Miami (Ohio) 14-13 and was on his way to an All-American career. As a senior, he starred for the 1978 Big-Ten champions. His 2,347 career receiving yards set a Big Ten record. In January 2017, he was elected into the College Football Hall of Fame.

While he was at Michigan State, Gibson also proved himself on the baseball diamond. He "tried baseball on a whim in 1978" and earned All-America honors after batting .390 and setting a school record by slamming 16 home runs.

Like Kirk Gibson, we, too, have to prove ourselves over and over again in our lives. To our teachers, our bosses or supervisors, that person we'd like to date, to our parents. We shouldn't be surprised at this; Jesus was constantly besieged by those seeking a sign through which he would prove himself to them.

For us, it's always the same question: "Am I good enough?" And yet, when it comes down to the most crucial situation in our lives, the answer is always a decisive and resounding "No!" Are we good enough to measure up to God? To deserve our salvation? Absolutely not; we never will be. That's why God sent Jesus to us.

The notion that only "good" people can be church members is a perversion of Jesus' entire ministry. Nobody is good enough — without Jesus. Everybody is good enough — with Jesus. That's not because of anything we have done for God, but because of what he has done for us. We have nothing to prove to God.

All this from a guy nobody recruited.
— Writer Joe Rexrode on Kirk Gibson's career at State

**The bad news is we can't prove to God's
satisfaction how good we are; the good news
is that because of Jesus we don't have to.**

DAY 67

HOW YOU SEE IT

Read John 20:11-18.

"Mary stood outside the tomb crying" (v. 11).

Should a flag have been thrown on the play that preserved one of the most thrilling upsets in MSU gridiron history? It depends on your perspective.

"NO. 1 VS. NO ONE." So declared T-shirts sold around Ann Arbor the week of the Michigan State game of Oct. 13, 1990. The Wolverines were ranked No. 1 while State was unranked. At least on paper, the game looked like a mismatch.

Sophomore tailback Tico Duckett, the league's Offensive MVP that season, didn't see it that way. "It didn't really make sense," he said. "Everybody thought Michigan was the powerhouse team, but we knew we were a powerhouse team, too."

The Spartans proved him right. State's offensive line — tackles Roosevelt Wagner and Jim Johnson, guards Eric Moten and Matt Keller, and center Jeff Pearson — dominated the supposedly physical Michigan defense. State rushed for 222 yards, getting 92 from Duckett and 93 from Hyland Hickson.

The game came down to the final seconds when the Wolverines scored with six ticks on the clock. That left MSU with a slim 28-27 lead; U-M went for the win. The quarterback lofted a strike to his receiver, who seemed to have cornerback Eddie Brown beaten.

Two different perspectives emerged from the play. The U-M receiver said, "When I got past him, he did what he could to stop me because it was do or die." Brown declared, "He got into me first, grabbed me, and pushed off. I pushed him away, he fell."

There was clearly contact on the play. The ball hit the receiver in the chest and bounced away. No flag was thrown.

After the game, the Michigan head coach said, "You guys saw it. It was ridiculous." Nevertheless, the ref's perspective prevailed. So did the final score of 28-27.

Your perspective goes a long way toward determining whether you slink through life amid despair, anger, and hopelessness or stride boldly through life with joy and hope. It's the difference between playing a game with vigor and determination or just going through the motions to get it over with.

Mary Magdalene is an excellent example. On that first Easter morning, she stood by Jesus' tomb crying with her heart broken because she still viewed everything through the perspective of Jesus' death. But how her attitude, her heart, and her life changed when she saw the morning through the perspective of Jesus' resurrection.

So it is with life and death for all of us. You can't avoid death, but you can determine how you perceive it. Is it fearful, dark, fraught with peril and uncertainty? Or is it a simple little passageway to glory, the light, and loved ones, an elevator ride to paradise?

It's a matter of perspective that depends totally on whether or not you're standing by Jesus' side when it arrives.

They have an argument.
— State head coach George Perles on U-M's calling for a flag

**Whether death is your worst enemy or
a solicitous chauffeur is a matter of perspective.**

HOLLYWOOD ENDING

Read Luke 24:1-12.

"Why do you look for the living among the dead? He is not here; he has risen!" (vv. 5, 6a)

With an ending that fit right in with the game's location near Hollywood, Michigan State won the 1956 Rose Bowl on a busted play as time ran out.

After an 8-1-0 season (See Devotion No. 14), Duffy Daugherty's Spartans headed for Pasadena to take on UCLA. So many students made the trip to support the team that railroad officials called it "the largest peace-time, non-military point-to-point mass movement by train in history."

The weather was clear and warm, the field in excellent shape on game day, Jan. 2. What resulted was "one of the most thrilling, tension-packed, fiercely contested" Rose Bowl games ever.

UCLA scored on the game's fifth play, but State shook off the rocky start and marched 79 yards in the second quarter. All-American quarterback Earl Morrall capped the drive with a 13-yard touchdown pass to fullback Clarence Peaks.

The game stayed knotted at seven until the second play of the fourth quarter when Morrall lateraled to Peaks, who drew up and completed a pass to end John "Thunder" Lewis. He went 50 yards to complete a 67-yard touchdown play.

When UCLA rallied to tie the game at 14, the stage was set for an unlikely Hollywood ending. With seven seconds left, Dave

Kaiser trotted out to try his first-ever field goal, from 41 yards, with Morrall the holder. It didn't go well. Kaiser was in the middle of a practice swing when the ball suddenly arrived in Morrall's hands. Startled, Morrall managed to get the ball down.

With no time to think about it, Kaiser could only act with his reflexes. He stepped back and swung through again. The kick on what was essentially a busted play was good. 17-14 State.

The world tells us that happy endings are for fairy tales and Hollywood's movies, that reality is Cinderella dying in childbirth and her prince getting killed in a peasant uprising. But that's just another of the world's lies.

The truth is that Jesus Christ has been producing happy endings for almost two millennia. That's because in Jesus lies the power to change and to rescue a life no matter how desperate the situation. Jesus is the master at putting shattered lives back together, of healing broken hearts and broken relationships, of resurrecting lost dreams.

And as for living happily ever after — God really means it. The greatest Hollywood ending of them all was written on a Sunday morning centuries ago when Jesus left a tomb and death behind. With faith in Jesus, your life can have that same ending. You live with God in peace, joy, and love — forever. The End.

A story-book finish that even Hollywood could not have duplicated with a script.
— Sports columnist Bill Corum on the end of the '56 Rose Bowl

Hollywood's happy endings are products of imagination; the happy endings Jesus produces are real and are yours for the asking.

DAY 69

FANCY FOOTWORK

Read Isaiah 52:7-12.

"How beautiful on the mountains are the feet of those who bring good news" (v. 7).

Reserve Spartan guard Jaimie Huffman became something of a national celebrity because of his footwear.

During the national championship season of 1978-79, Huffman saw action in nine games, scoring two points and nabbing three rebounds. His moment of fame came in State's first game of the 1979 NCAA Tournament, a 95-64 rout of Lamar.

Late in the game, Jud Heathcote emptied his bench. In Huffman's first few seconds of action, a Lamar player stepped on one of his shoes and his heel came out. "I tied my laces in a double knot so they wouldn't come off," Huffman recalled. "The game was going on and I was trying to get my laces undone."

Meanwhile, Heathcote was hollering at him to get down the court with one shoe. Huffman tried that, "but it was like I was on ice." So he stopped and took his time to get the shoe on properly.

NBC commentator Al McGuire noticed State playing with only four bodies. He spotted Huffman by himself busy at work with his footwear and started calling him "Shoes" Huffman. When Huffman scored his first and only basket of the season and went to the line for a free throw, the cameras zeroed in on . . . his shoes.

Back home in East Lansing, a sign on a dormitory declared, "Welcome home, Shoes." The campus bookstore even sold some

"Shoes" memorabilia.

Huffman also played in the semifinals, a 101-67 romp past Penn. After the game, State SID Fred Stabley told Shoes he was wanted back on the court for an interview. It was the *NBC* crew.

Gerald Gilkie, Hoffman's roommate on the road, told Shoes he was going to pull his shorts down the next time he played so people could start calling him "Shorts."

Except when we're out shopping for new shoes, we rarely pay much attention to our feet. Throw athlete's foot, corns, bunions, or ingrown toenails into the mix, however, and those aching digits make us much more aware of them and how important they are.

Even if we are flattered when someone tells us how lovely certain of our body parts are, we probably regard as slightly strange someone's commenting on how pretty our feet are. Especially if we're men and don't have the advantage of painted toenails.

But even Jehovah himself waxes poetic about our pretty feet when we are hotfooting about delivering the good news of salvation through Jesus Christ. We are commissioned by our Lord not to prop our feet up, but rather to put those feet — flat or otherwise — onto the ground and share with others God's life-changing message of redemption through Christ.

The feet of the gospel's messenger are beautiful because they bear the bearer of the most beautiful message of all: Jesus saves.

When I got to the floor, it was Dick Enberg and [Al] McGuire, and I was live on NBC. *That was pretty incredible.*
— Jaimie Huffman on being interviewed after the NCAA semifinal

Our feet are beautiful when they take us to people
who need the message of salvation in Jesus.

DAY 70

THE OPPORTUNITY

Read Colossians 4:2-6.

[M]ake the most of every opportunity" (v. 5b).

All Greg Jones asked of his coaches was an opportunity to get on the field. When he got it, he made MSU gridiron history.

A linebacker, Jones finished his State career in 2010 as one of the greatest players in the program's history. He was the second Spartan to lead the team in tackles four straight seasons. (Dan Bass (1976-79) was the first.) He was only the fourth two-time consensus first-team All-America in program history. (George Webster, Bubba Smith, and Lorenzo White are the others.)

Unlikely as it may seem, Jones wasn't highly recruited coming out of high school. The only Big Ten school to offer him a scholarship was Minnesota. He took it. But prior to National Signing Day, Minnesota fired its head coach, and Mark Dantonio took over at State. The head Spartan had recruited Jones when he was at Cincinnati and convinced him to come to East Lansing.

Jones knew he had the opportunity of a lifetime, but he arrived on campus with very tempered expectations. As Jones recalled it, "I remember talking to the special teams coach and just asking him a whole lot: 'Can I just get on the field and make a play?'"

Jones did indeed get on the field. He wound up starting 46 of his 52 career games, including forty straight at one point. His first game was at home on Sept. 1, 2007, a 55-18 romp over Alabama-Birmingham. As he prepared to run onto the field, Jones paused

SPARTANS

for a moment in the tunnel to take it all in. It didn't last long. One of the veterans had a note of warning for the rookie: "You got to keep moving." "I was like, 'Oh, yeah, yeah,'" Jones said.

Dantonio and Jones' position coach, Mike Tressel, both figured Jones would have an outstanding career, but neither coach realistically expected the greatness they came to see. Greg Jones simply made the absolute most of the opportunity he was given.

An opportunity like a college football career usually gives us only one shot at it. Miss the chance and it's gone forever. The house you wanted that came on the market; that chance for promotion that opened up, the accidental meeting with that person you've been attracted to from a distance: If the opportunity comes, you have to grab it right now or you may well miss it.

This doesn't hold true in our faith life, however. Salvation through Jesus Christ is not a one-and-done deal. As long as we live, every day and every minute of our life, the opportunity to turn to Jesus is always with us. We have unlimited access to the saving grace of our Lord and Savior.

As with any opportunity, though, we must avail ourselves of it. That is, salvation is ours for the taking but we must take it. The inherent tragedy of an unsaved life thus is not that the opportunity for salvation was withdrawn or unavailable, but that it was squandered.

When I first came here, I told linebackers coach Mike Tressel, 'I just want an opportunity.'
— Greg Jones on starting out at Michigan State

**We have the opportunity for salvation
through Jesus Christ at any time.**

UNDERDOGS

Read 1 Samuel 17:17-50.

"David said to the Philistine, . . . 'This day the Lord will hand you over to me, and I'll strike you down'" (vv. 45-46).

We make a lot of people look foolish." Never so much, however, as the day State played without its star QB and slew a giant.

Two-time All-American center Jack Allen delivered his terse assessment of his football team following the Ohio State game of 2015. It was, in retrospect, entirely accurate because the Spartans entered the game as 13-point underdogs. Considering the circumstances, the point spread probably should have been more.

On one sideline of their home field stood the 3rd-ranked Buckeyes, winners of 23 straight games and 30 straight Big Ten contests. Across the way gathered the 9th-ranked Spartans, who, in addition to the usual difficulties involved in facing an undefeated team that was the hands-down pick to win the national title, had a problem most observers felt rendered them unable to compete: Senior quarterback Connor Cook had a sprained left shoulder and couldn't play for the first time in 37 games. His replacements, junior Tyler O'Conner and sophomore Damion Terry, would thus get the first significant playing time of their careers.

In other words, the Spartans had the Buckeyes right where they wanted them. As head coach Mark Dantonio said, "We came in with something to prove. When you have that, you have a little chip on your shoulder and play a little better."

Indeed. The underdogs dominated both sides of the line of scrimmage. They ran the ball 51 times and held it for 38:10. Ohio State could manage only 45 snaps the whole game with a measly five first downs and a pitiful 132 yards of total offense.

Thus, as time expired, Michael Geiger, all 5-foot-8 and 185 lbs of him, became the biggest man on campus when he booted a 41-yard field for the 17-14 Spartan win.

Goliath had run head-on into little David once again.

You probably don't gird your loins, pick up a slingshot and some smooth, round river rocks, and go out to battle ill-tempered giants regularly. You do, however, fight each day to make some economic and social progress and to keep the ones you love safe, sheltered, and protected. Armed only with your pluck, your knowledge, your wits, and your hustle, in many ways you are an underdog; the best you can hope for is that the world is indifferent. You need all the weapons you can get.

How about using the ultimate weapon David had: the absolute, unshakable conviction that when he tackled opposition of any size, he would prevail. He knew this because he did everything for God's glory and therefore God was in his corner. If you imitate David's lifestyle by glorifying God in everything you do, then God is there for you when you need him.

Who's the underdog then?

The Spartans relish the role of underdog like no powerhouse program.
— ESPN *on Michigan State's 2015 football team*

Living to glorify God is the lifestyle
of a champion, not an underdog.

WHAT A DIFFERENCE

Read Daniel 3.

*"We want you to know, O king, that we will not serve
your gods or worship the image of gold you have set up"
(v. 18).*

College football in East Lansing was quite different back in the days of the World War I era and the 1920s.

In those times before scholarships, the rules governing eligibility and amateurism were different: there really weren't any. College players often played some pro football to earn living money. For instance, Brownie Springer was a star quarterback for Michigan Agricultural College (The name was different then.) in 1915 and '16. The only help he received "was a job at the gym and meals at training table. . . . I believe I got $.40 an hour." So he and many other MAC players played for pay on Sundays. It was worth his while as he received $150 plus expenses. "I never could have finished school otherwise," he said.

The Aggies (The nickname was different then.) played in a totally different conference back then. Ralph Young, "a lovable, roly-poly extrovert" who was a master at public relations, coached football at MAC (which became Michigan State College in 1925) from 1923-27. Young joined with the coaches at Notre Dame and Marquette to form the Central Collegiate Conference in 1926. For many years, it rivaled the Big Ten in every sport but football.

What was celebrated back then was different, too, as it wasn't just football wins. A defeat of Michigan in baseball in 1925 touched off a wild celebration. Led by Skinny Skellenger, "a cheerleader with madcap propensities," the students set fire to the old center-field section of bleachers. The groundskeeper "barely saved his beloved power lawnmover," the school's first. The police had to contend with Skellenger, who climbed up a telephone pole and bombarded unwitting passersby with rotten eggs.

Much is different today from those old days, but one key aspect of Christian living has not changed: the call from a risen Christ to be different amid a secular society that constantly pressures us to conform to its principles and values. Therein lies the great conflict of the Christian life in contemporary America.

But how many of us really consider that even in our secular society we struggle to conform? We are all geeks in a sense. We can never truly conform because we were not created by God to live in such a sin-filled world in the first place. Thus, when Christ calls us to be different by following and espousing Christian beliefs, principles, and practices, he is summoning us to the lifestyle we were born for.

The most important step in being different for Jesus is realizing and admitting what we really are: We are children of God; we are Christians. Only secondarily are we citizens of a secular world. That world both scorns and disdains us for being different; Jesus both praises and loves us for it.

[Football players] switched freely from school to school.
 — *Fred W. Stabley on one of the differences about early college football*

The lifestyle Jesus calls us to is different from that of the world, but it is the way we were born to live.

DAY 73

TEAM PLAYERS

Read 1 Corinthians 12:4-13, 27-31.

"Now to each one the manifestation of the Spirit is given for the common good" (v. 7).

Half a world away from East Lansing, the Spartans discovered a profound definition of what it means to be part of a team.

When *ESPN* called coach Tom Izzo with a proposal for a game in Germany at Air Force headquarters, he didn't hesitate. After all, one of the most moving events of his life had been the 2011 game against North Carolina on the deck of the USS Carl Vinson.

Thus, on Friday, Nov. 9, 2012, the Spartans played the UConn Huskies. The game was memorable in itself, but what the players and coaches experienced prior to the tipoff may very well be what they will always remember most.

After landing in Germany on Nov. 7, the teams made the 90-minute drive to Ramstein Air Base. The game of 2011 had been a celebratory event; this time the mood was much more solemn.

That's because the first stop was at the base medical facilities. During a tutorial explaining the base's mission, MSU assistant coach Mike Garland asked what the average age of the wounded and injured was. The response was 20 to 21. To be sure the point was made, Garland observed that was the same age as his players.

As if that were not sobering enough, the players visited the base hospital where Izzo and team captains Derrick Nix and Russell Byrd met an excited 1SG Davidson Christmas. He had been

SPARTANS

seriously wounded in Afghanistan and was being shipped back to the States. To the trio's surprise, he wasn't happy about it.

He explained that he wanted to wrap up his mission with his team. He didn't want to leave anyone behind or let them fend for themselves. He wanted above all else to be with his team.

"It hit me," said Izzo. 1SG Christmas "wants to be with his team. We talk about sacrifice in sports, but this is the ultimate sacrifice."

Most accomplishments are the result of teamwork, whether it's a military mission, a basketball team, the running of a household, or the completion of a project at work. Disparate talents and gifts work together for the common good and the greater goal.

A church works the same way. At its most basic, a church is a team that has been and is being assembled by God. A shared faith drives the team members and impels them toward shared goals. As a successful Spartans basketball team must have a point guard and a strong forward, so must a church be composed of people with different spiritual and personal gifts. The result is something greater than everyone involved.

What makes a church team different from other group efforts is that the individual endeavors are expended for the glory of God and not for the glory of self. The nature of a church member's particular talents doesn't matter; what matters is that those talents are used as part of God's team.

It's tough to leave this team here. I'm disappointed.
— 1SG Davidson Christmas on returning stateside

A church is a team of people using their various talents and gifts for God, the source of all those abilities to begin with.

CHEAP TRICKS

Read Acts 19:11-20.

"The evil spirit answered them, 'Jesus I know, and I know about Paul, but who are you?'" (v. 15)

A wily football coach once took advantage of a loophole in the rules to trick State. The Spartans' wily coach responded with a trick of his own.

The biggest win of State's 6-2 season of 1935 was a 12-7 defeat of Temple, coached by the legendary Glenn "Pop" Warner. The Owls had won fifteen straight when Coach Charlie Bachman's squad arrived in Philadelphia for the Nov. 2 game.

In those days before extensive pre-game scouting, Warner used a gimmick to confound the opposing team. Football teams of the time weren't required to have numbers on their uniforms and helmets. Warner lined up his team with the center over the ball, nine players in a line one yard behind the center, and one back, the fullback, about five yards behind this group.

The Temple players then stood in formation with their heads down. It was impossible to tell a lineman from a back. They then shifted quickly into position with the backs already in the spot they needed to be. With a quick snap, the defense had no chance to overcome its confusion and counter the formation.

Bachman, who had a 70-34-10 record from 1933-46 at State, came up with a trick of his own. He gave each of the two tackles and two guards a piece of black chalk. After the first play was over, the four Temple backs had big black X's on the front of their jerseys and on their sleeves. The backs had been identified.

Bachman had one more trick to play. Despite trailing 7-0, he started a team of reserves in the second half. When he put his starters back in to start the fourth quarter, they were fresh. All-American fullback Art Brandstatter ripped off a 59-yard touchdown run and set up the winning score with a run to the 3.

Scam artists are everywhere — and they love trick plays. An e-mail encourages you to send money to some foreign country to get rich. That guy at your front door offers to resurface your driveway at a ridiculously low price. A TV ad promises a pill to help you lose weight without diet or exercise.

You've been around; you check things out before deciding. The same approach is necessary with spiritual matters, too, because false religions and bogus Christian denominations abound. The key is what any group does with Jesus. Is he the son of God, the ruler of the universe, and the only way to salvation? If not, then what the group espouses is something other than the true Word of God.

The good news about Jesus does indeed sound too good to be true, but the only catch is that there is no catch. When it comes to salvation through Jesus Christ, there's no trick lurking in the fine print. There's just the truth, right there for you to see.

Sid Wagner walk[ed] up to one of their backs, turn[ed] him around and made a big black X on his shirt with the man in complete amazement.
— *End Frank Gaines on Coach Charlie Bachman's trick vs. Temple*

God's promises through Jesus sound too good to be true, but the only catch is that there is no catch.

VIRTUAL REALITY

Read Habakkuk 1:2-11.

"Why do you make me look at injustice? Why do you tolerate wrong? Destruction and violence are before me; there is strife, and conflict abounds" (v. 3).

The final score of 10-7 seems to indicate a tense, thrilling nail-biter of a football game. In this case, though, reality was something quite different.

That 10-7 tally comes from the MSU-Ohio State game of 2011. It was truly a big win for the Spartans on their way to the Big Ten Championship Game and an 11-win season.

The game *should* have been close considering the principals involved, but it really wasn't thanks to mistakes by the Spartan offense and an absolutely dominating performance by the MSU defense. Quarterback Kirk Cousins acknowledged the final score should have been much more lopsided. "We didn't finish our drives. We could have had 20 to 25-plus points," he said.

For MSU's defense, which justified its lofty perch as the nation's top-ranked bunch, the ten points the offense managed were quite enough to ensure a win. The Buckeyes "were a complete mess" on the offensive side of the ball. They managed only 178 total yards including a pitiful 35 rushing yards on 39 attempts.

The smothering defenders posted nine sacks. Linebacker Max Bullough had nine tackles, including one of these sacks. Linebackers Denicos Allen and Chris Norman had two sacks each.

SPARTANS

Thus, Cousins' 33-yard touchdown pass to B.J. Cunningham in the first quarter provided a 7-0 lead that seemed to be much bigger as the MSU defense overwhelmed the Buckeyes. Dan Conroy's 50-yard field goal in the fourth quarter that gave MSU a 10-0 lead effectively ended the party. Buckeye fans knew it, raining down a hearty chorus of boos on their hapless team.

Only an Ohio State touchdown with ten seconds left made the game look closer than it really was.

As is the case in football, sometimes in life reality isn't what it seems. In our violent and convulsive times, we must confront the possibility of a new reality: that we are helpless in the face of anarchy; that injustice, destruction, and violence are pandemic in and symptomatic of our modern age. Anarchy seems to be winning, and the system of standards, values, and institutions we have cherished appears to be crumbling while we watch.

But we should not be deceived or disheartened. God is in fact the arch-enemy of chaos, the creator of order and goodness and the architect of all of history. God is in control. We often misinterpret history as the record of mankind's accomplishments — which it isn't — rather than the unfolding of God's plan — which it is. That plan has a clearly defined end: God will make everything right. In that day reality will be exactly what it seems to be.

The Spartans should have won this game by a much more comfortable final score.
— ESPN's *Brian Bennett on MSU's 'close' defeat of Ohio State*

**The forces of good and decency often seem
helpless before evil's power, but don't be fooled:
God is in control and will set things right.**

SIGHT UNSEEN

Read 2 Corinthians 5:6-10.

"We live by faith, not by sight" (v. 7).

Bobby Williams didn't see the play that won his first game as Michigan State's head football coach.

After leading the Spartans to a 9-2 season, a No.-9 ranking, and a second-place finish in the Big Ten in 1999, Nick Saban accepted an offer from LSU to take over the Tigers' program and took off for Baton Rouge. The team, meanwhile, still had a date on Jan. 1 with Florida in the Citrus Bowl.

Williams, Saban's assistant head coach and running backs boss, was named the interim head coach for the bowl game. What was already a tumultuous time got even more unsettled when the players launched an organized effort to have Williams named the permanent head coach, hinting at a boycott of the bowl game.

Williams' response was to tell the MSU powers-that-be that he wanted to be interviewed for the job. Four days after Saban had left, Williams had his meeting. One overriding theme carried the day for Saban's assistant: the need for continuity. That evening after midnight he was hired with the lone proviso that his assistant coaches stay, too.

Williams' debut was a thriller. With only a few seconds left on the clock, the Spartans lined up for a 39-yard field goal that would win it 37-34. The kicker was All-American Paul Edinger, who still holds the school record for highest career field-goal percentage.

SPARTANS

He was such a lock that his teammates nicknamed him "Money."

As usual, his kick was good, dead center even. He didn't see it. As soon as the ball left his foot, Edinger took off for the dressing room to celebrate. Williams also knew the kick was good the moment it took flight, but his players dumped a Gatorade bucket on him before the ball reached the crossbar. They knocked off his glasses in the process; distracted and with his eyesight uncorrected, Williams never saw the game winner.

To close our eyes or to be engulfed suddenly by total darkness plunges us into a world in which we struggle to function. Our world and our place in it are built on our eyesight, so much so that we tout "Seeing is believing." If we can't see it, we don't believe it. Perhaps the most famous proponent of this attitude was the disciple Thomas, who refused to believe Jesus had risen from the dead until he saw the proof for himself.

But our sight carries us only so far because its usefulness is restricted to the physical world. Eyesight has no place in spiritual matters. We don't "see" God; we don't "see" Jesus; we don't "see" God at work in the physical world. And yet we know God; we know Jesus; we know God is in control. We "know" all that because as the children of God, we live by faith and not by sight.

Looking through the eyes of faith, we come to understand that believing is seeing.

[The players] made a happy mess of a head coach who didn't mind that he never saw [Paul]Edinger's kick sail high above the crossbar.
— Sportswriter Lynn Henning in Spartan Seasons II

In God's physical world, seeing is believing;
in God's spiritual world, believing is seeing.

DAY 77

ON THE MONEY

Read Luke 16:1-15.

"You cannot serve both God and money" (v. 13b).

Once upon a time, the budget was so tight for Michigan State baseball that head coach Danny Litwhiler hosted a wine and cheese party to raise funds and encouraged his players to eat a good breakfast at home before a road trip.

Litwhiler coached the Spartans from 1964-82 at a time when baseball's budget was bare bones. He won 489 games, the most of any coach in MSU history, and two Big Ten titles. Three of his squads earned berths in the NCAA Tournament.

But money was always a problem. For Litwhiler, an essential part of the program was an annual ten-day spring trip to Florida. His team escaped the Michigan weather for some outdoor games against good baseball schools. Paying for it was quite a trick. The team usually stayed in a motel with fuzzy black-and-white TVs, small bathrooms, and a rate of $4 per person with two players in a bed. A Lansing auto dealer arranged on-site cars for the squad.

In the spring of '73, Lutwhiler ran across an idea to raise money for the Florida trip: a wine and cheese party. He arranged for both the wines and the cheese to be donated, raised about $2,000, and realized some public-relations benefits for the program.

Paying for the food on road trips for hearty, hungry baseball players was always a concern, too. The usual format for in-state road games was to encourage everyone to eat a good breakfast at home. Sandwich essentials such as ham and cheese, mustard, and mayo were carried on the bus for lunch. After the games, the usual stop was a Kentucky Fried Chicken.

For overnight trips, Litwhiler arranged for airlines-style hot plates from the school's food services. The Coca-Cola company donated drinks. To save money on the overnight trips, the team often stayed at the host school's student union.

Unlike Danny Litwhiler's situation, you may have found that having a little too much money at the end of the month may be as bothersome — if not as worrisome — as having a little too much month at the end of the money. What are you to do with that "disposable income"? The investment possibilities are bewildering: stocks, bonds, real estate, managed futures, hedge funds, commodities (even pork bellies), on and on.

You take your money seriously, as well you should. Jesus, too, took money seriously, warning us frequently of its dangers. Money itself is not evil; its peril lies in the ease with which it can usurp God's rightful place as the master of our lives.

Certainly in our age and society, we often fall into the trap of measuring people by how much money they have (or at least seem to have). But like our other talents, gifts, and resources, money should primarily be used for God's purposes. God's love must touch not only our hearts but our wallets also.

How much of your wealth are you investing with God?

The baseball team's Florida trip was an exercise in austerity.
— Sportswriter Lynn Henning

**Your attitude about money says much
about your attitude toward God.**

FAMILY TRADITION

Read Mark 7:1-13.

"You have let go of the commands of God and are holding on to the traditions of men" (v. 8).

The composer of one of Michigan State's greatest traditions — the school's fight song — died before he knew it would achieve such a revered status.

On Oct. 18, 1913, Michigan Agricultural College beat Michigan in football for the first time. (See Devotion No. 27.) After the game, the MAC students and fans paraded through Ann Arbor celebrating their victory by singing — of all things — Michigan's fight song. The next week, the Aggies beat Wisconsin, and despite the defeat, Wisconsin's fans jubilantly sang their fight song.

Francis Lankey, MAC Class of 1916, was a civil engineering major and a cheerleader. He had been dismayed by MAC fans' singing of Michigan's fight song and impressed by the Wisconsin fight song. He decided MAC needed one of its own.

An accomplished pianist and composer, Lankey teamed with engineering senior Arthur L. Sayles in 1915 to compose a fight song for the college. Nobody paid much attention.

In 1919, Lankey was an instructor for the Army Air Corps when he was killed in a plane crash. Several months later, a girlfriend published his MAC song. Members of the football team sold copies of it for 50 cents at the Homecoming pep rally to raise some money. When they sold all 770 copies in less than 30 minutes,

SPARTANS

"everyone knew the Fight Song was a winner."

In 1920, the Military Band played what would become MSU's official fight song at football games and other sporting events for the first time. It has been played ever since with only slight variations of the words. On the occasion of its 100th anniversary in 2015, the song's title was changed to "Victory for MSU."

You encounter traditions practically everywhere in your life. MSU has them. So does your workplace. Your family may have a particular way of celebrating Christmas or Easter.

Your church undoubtedly has traditions also. A particular type of music, for instance. Or the order of worship.

Jesus knew all about religious tradition; after all, he grew up in the Church. He understood, though, the danger that lay in allowing tradition to become a religion in and of itself, and in his encounter with the Pharisees, Jesus rebuked them for just that.

Jesus changed everything that the world had ever known about faith. This included the traditions that had gradually arisen to define the way the Jews of his day worshipped. Jesus declared that those who truly worship God do not do so by simply observing various traditions, but rather by establishing a meaningful, deep-seated personal relationship with him.

Tradition in our faith life is useful only when it helps to draw us closer to God.

On the banks of the Red Cedar, There's a school that's known to all; Its speciality is winning, And those Spartans play good ball.
— Lines from 'Victory for MSU'

Religious tradition has value only when it serves to strengthen our relationship with God.

YOU DECIDE

Read Acts 16:22-34.

"[The jailer] asked, 'Sirs, what must I do to be saved?'
They replied, 'Believe in the Lord Jesus, and you will be
saved'" (vv. 30-31).

As a freshman, Evan Jones decided to use his hair to make a statement about his commitment to the Spartans.

Jones completed his football career at MSU as a senior in 2016. He was a three-year letterwinner at defensive end, working his way through the process head coach Mark Dantonio and his staff preferred. He took a redshirt season, experimented at a couple of positions, worked his way onto the field on special teams and as a backup, and then took over the starting spot as a senior. "That's the rule rather than the exception," said co-defensive coordinator Mike Tressel about Jones' career path at State. "You pay your dues and you learn what we're all about, about Spartan toughness."

Part of Jones' learning curve in East Lansing involved his hair, which was the reason he got a late start at football in high school. His school's head coach had a strict edict: No player could have hair below his ears.

That didn't sit too well with Jones, who sported locks down past his shoulder. "The hair was pretty long," he said. "It was definitely over a foot." He had no interest in getting it cut, though the head coach bugged him daily about "turn[ing] in his skateboard for a pair of shoulder pads."

SPARTANS

The head coach was in a bind. He was coaching in West Lafayette, Ohio, population 2,300. Jones was fast growing into a 6-foot-5 athlete, not a commodity the school's hallways were packed with. The coach eventually relented and a shaggy Jones played.

He arrived at State in 2012 "as a tight end who looked ready for a motorcycle rally — long hair, well-inked arms and a shaggy beard." Early on, though, Jones decided that the hair had to go as a way of signaling his dedication to the MSU football team.

As with Evan Jones and his haircut, the decisions you have made along the way have shaped your life at pivotal moments. Some decisions you made suddenly and carelessly; some you made carefully and deliberately; some were forced upon you. You may have discovered to your dismay that some of those spur-of-the-moment decisions have turned out better than your carefully considered ones.

Of all your life's decisions, however, none is more important than one you cannot ignore: What have you done with Jesus? Even in his time, people chose to follow Jesus or to reject him, and nothing has changed. As it was with the Roman jailer, the decision must still be made and nobody can make it for you. Ignoring Jesus won't work either; that is, in fact, a decision, and neither he nor the consequences of your decision will go away.

Carefully considered or spontaneous: how you arrive at a decision for Jesus doesn't matter. All that matters is that you get there.

It was a good decision for sure.
— Evan Jones on cutting his hair

A decision for Jesus may be spontaneous or considered; what counts is that you make it.

DAY 80

OF GENTLE MEN

Read John 2:12-17.

"He made a whip out of cords, and drove all from the temple area . . .; he scattered the coins of the money changers and overturned their tables" (v. 15).

The MAC football team once received a quite stern lecture about being gentlemen from an unexpected source.

John Macklin, head football coach for the Michigan Agricultural College Aggies (1911-15), was a master at motivation and public relations. In the fall of 1913, he used his PR talents to motivate his players by making preseason training more enjoyable. He prevailed upon a friend to allow his team to use a cottage in the middle of what was then Pine Lake (now Lake Lansing). The owner even threw in the services of his chef and provided food for the fifteen players, the coach, and the manager.

The team conducted its drills on a field on the mainland. They usually rode the train to the site but sometimes rode in a real novelty: Macklin's electric automobile.

The team's manager, Merrill Fuller, had a special memory of the trip. He recounted that the players discovered a sailing boat anchored at a dock and proceeded to take it on an extended cruise of the lake. Unfortunately, they didn't return it.

As Fuller recalled it, on Sunday morning they were all relaxing on the cottage's sun porch when a rowboat approached. In it was Gladys Olds, the daughter of automobile pioneer R.E. Olds, to whom the sailboat belonged. She asked who was in charge; the players quickly pointed to Fuller.

Fuller said, "She stood up in the boat and delivered a splendid lecture about the difference between gentlemen and vandals." Then she sat down and ordered the boat to be rowed away. Fuller made sure the players returned the boat pronto.

It was so in 1913 and it is so today: We expect gentlemanly behavior — both on and off the field — from the young men representing the Spartan football team. Gentle men are frequently misunderstood by those who fail to appreciate their inner strength. But Jesus' rampage through the Jerusalem temple illustrates the perils of underestimating a determined gentleman.

A gentleman treats other people kindly, respectfully, and justly, and conducts himself ethically in all situations. A gentleman doesn't lack resolve or backbone. Instead, he determines to live in a way that is exceedingly difficult in our selfish, me-first society; he lives the lifestyle God desires for us all.

Included in that mode of living is the understanding that the best way to have a request honored is to make it civilly, with a smile. God works that way too. He could bully you and boss you around; you couldn't stop him. But instead, he gently requests your attention and politely waits for the courtesy of a reply.

When [Gladys Olds] finished, I proceeded in a hurry to get the boat back to where it belonged — and in good condition.
— Team Manager Merrill Fuller on the effect of Olds' lecture

God is a gentleman, soliciting your attention
politely and then patiently waiting for you
to give him the courtesy of a reply.

QUIET TIME

Read 1 Kings 19:1-13.

"And after the earthquake a fire, but the Lord was not in the fire: and after the fire a still small voice" (v. 12 KJV).

What Mike Brkovich remembered most about his clutch free throws against Iowa was how quiet Jenison Field House was.

Brkovich joined Magic Johnson, Greg Kelser, Jay Vincent, and Terry Donnelly in the starting lineup for the 1979 national champions. Dubbed "The Golden Arm" by head coach Jud Heathcote, Brkovich was the first Canadian ever to start in NCAA's Division I championship game.

On Jan. 20, 1979, Michigan State hosted Iowa, which would finish the season ranked number 20 and tied with the Spartans and Purdue atop the Big Ten standings. As expected, the game was a thriller. With three seconds left, State trailed 65-63, but a controversial foul call sent Brkovich to the line for two shots.

The Hawkeyes called two timeouts to freeze him, the second one coming after Brkovich had made the first shot. "Each time in the huddle," Brkovich recalled, [head coach] "Jud [Heathcote] would talk about what we were going to do after I made the free throws. Just as I was leaving the huddle before the final free throw, Coach told me, 'You'll make it.'"

Brkovich did, sending the game into overtime. Interestingly, the sophomore forward remembered little about the free throws. "They went in," he said. "I was nervous."

SPARTANS

What he always recalled about the moment was the eerie quiet that descended upon Jenison Field House as he stood at the line. The place "was always so loud, and when I stepped to the line, there was dead silence," Bkokvich said.

That silence lasted only until Brkovich's free throws sent the game into overtime. The riotous racket continued into the extra period as the Spartans rolled to an 83-72 win.

Indoors, the television blares, the ring tone sounds off, the dishwasher rattles. Outdoors, the roar, beeps, and honks of traffic and car horns assault your ears, a siren screams until you wince, and everybody shouts to be heard above the din.

We live in a noisy world. Strangely enough, the most powerful voice of all — the one whose voice spoke the universe into being — does not join in the cacophony. We would expect Almighty God to speak in a thunderous roar, complete with lightning, that forces us to cover our ears and fall to our knees in dread.

Instead, God patiently waits for us to turn to him, nudging us gently with a still small voice. Thus, in the serenity of quiet time expressly set aside for God, and not in the daily tumult, do we find God and discover something rather remarkable: that God's being with us is not remarkable at all. He's always there; we just can't hear him most of the time over the world's noise.

It's a lot better to be seen than heard. The sun is the most powerful thing I know of, and it doesn't make much noise.

— Bear Bryant

**God speaks in a whisper, not a shout,
so we must listen carefully,
or we will miss his voice altogether.**

DAY 82

YOU NEVER KNOW

Read Acts 26:1-20.

"[I]n all Judea, and to the Gentiles also, I preached that they should repent and turn to God" (v. 20).

You never know just how a kid may wind up playing football for a particular school. Blake Ezor, for instance, landed in East Lansing because of a Las Vegas casino baccarat dealer.

Ezor is one of the greatest of Spartan running backs. From 1986-89, he rushed for 3,749 yards, which remains in the record book as the fourth-best standard. Ezor is also fourth with 800 career rushes and fourth in rushing touchdowns with 34.

Ezor had his greatest game as a Spartan in 1989, his senior season. In a 76-14 crushing of Northwestern on Nov. 18, he set a Big Ten record by scoring six touchdowns. His 36 points was also a conference record. During 1987's run to the Rose Bowl, State was struggling against Indiana until Ezor blew the game open with a 90-yard kickoff return.

So how did this "wiry kid with blond hair and a touch of Dennis the Menace about him" who hailed from Las Vegas wind up at Michigan State? When head coach George Perles was with the Pittsburgh Steelers, the team took an annual post-season vacation to Las Vegas. A Pittsburgh native ran the baccarat table that was a favorite of the coaches and players. His name was Bernie Ezor.

Several years later, that Vegas dealer called Perles to tell him his son was a speedster State should take a look at. Perles had heard that song before from a well-intentioned parent, but he asked assistant Ted Guthard to review some film and check young Ezor out. Guthard issued a one-word scouting report: "Wow."

Ezor was on his way to State. You just never know.

In your life, you, too, never know exactly how events will transpire. In truth, you never know what you can do until you want to bad enough or until — like Paul — you have to because God insists. Serving in the military, maybe even in combat. Standing by a friend while everyone else unjustly excoriates her. Undergoing agonizing medical treatment and managing to smile. You never know what life will demand of you.

It's that way too in your relationship with God. As Paul, the dogged persecutor of first-century Christians, discovered, you never know what God will ask of you. You can know that God expects you to be faithful; thus, you must be willing to trust him even when he calls you to tasks that appear daunting and beyond your abilities.

You can respond faithfully and confidently to whatever it is God calls you to do for him. That's because even though you never know what lies ahead, you can know with absolutely certainty that God will lead you and will provide what you need. As it was with the Israelites, God will never lead you into the wilderness and then leave you there.

There's one word to describe baseball: You never know.

— *Yogi Berra*

**You never know what God will ask you to do,
but you always know he will provide
everything you need to do it.**

TEN TO REMEMBER

Read Exodus 20:1-17.

*"God spoke all these words: 'I am the Lord your God . . . .
You shall have no other gods before me'" (vv. 1, 3).*

With the 2015 regular season completed, *ESPN*'s Dan Murphy chose the ten plays that propelled the Spartans to the most successful football campaign in history: twelve wins, the Big Ten championship, and a berth in the College Football Playoff.

In chronological order they were:

#1) Malik McDowell's fourth-down stuff of Oregon on Sept. 12. The play capped a five-play MSU goal-line stand from inside the 5-yard line (31-28 win). #2) Cornerback Arjen Colquhoun's break-up of a fourth-down pass against Purdue on Oct. 3 (24-21 win).

#3) R.J. Shelton's over-the-defender catch of a Connor Cook pass late in the Rutgers game of Oct. 10. The spectacular grab sparked a 10-play, 76-yard game-winning drive (31-24 win). #4) Fullback Trevor Pendleton's 74-yard rumble to set up a State touchdown against Michigan on Oct. 17. The score pulled the Spartans to within 23-21 and "set up the craziest finish in program history."

#5) That "craziest finish" against Michigan. Jalen Watts-Jackson scooped up a bumbled punt in the closing seconds and ran 38 yards for the game winner (27-23 win). #6) The last-minute touchdown pass by Nebraska on Nov. 7. MSU players said the loss served as a wake-up call for a defense that the Cornhuskers riddled for 39 points (39-38 loss).

#7) Gerald Holmes' game-tying score from the 2-yard line versus Ohio State on Nov. 21. #8) Michael Geiger's dramatic 41-yard field goal as time expired that beat OSU (17-14 win).

#9) The interception in the end zone by Demetrious Cox in the Big Ten championship game of Dec. 5. The play kept State from falling behind Iowa 10-0. #10) LJ Scott's heroic championship-winning run through five defenders against Iowa (16-13 win).

For MSU fans, these are indeed ten to remember for the ages.

You have your list and you're ready to go: a gallon of paint and a water hose from the hardware store; chips, peanuts, and sodas from the grocery store for watching tonight's football game with your buddies; the concert tickets. Your list helps you remember.

God also made a list once of things he wanted you to remember; it's called the Ten Commandments. Just as your list reminds you to do something, so does God's list remind you of how you are to act in your dealings with other people and with him.

A life dedicated to Jesus is a life devoted to relationships, and God's list emphasizes that the social life and the spiritual life of the faithful cannot be sundered. God's relationship to you is one of unceasing, unqualified love, and you are to mirror that divine love in your relationships with others.

In case you forget, you have a list.

Society today treats the Ten Commandments as if they were the ten suggestions. Never compromise on right or wrong.
— Former college baseball coach Gordie Gillespie

God's top ten list is a set of instructions
on how you are to conduct yourself
with other people and with him.

TAKING A CHANCE

Read Matthew 4:18-22.

"[A]nd immediately they left the boat and their father and followed him" (v. 22).

Mark Dantonio decided it was time to take a chance. It paid off.

The 7-0 Spartans found themselves in a real catfight when they tangled with the Northwestern Wildcats on Oct. 23, 2010. In the second quarter, they trailed 17-0.

The game marked Dantonio's first return to the field since he had suffered a heart attack after the Notre Dame game of Sept. 18. (See Devotion No. 42.) His presence on the sideline became key early in the fourth quarter.

State trailed 24-14 and faced fourth-and-6 at the Wildcat 31. A field goal was problematical because of a stiff headwind. Still, the Spartans lined up to try it before Dantonio called a timeout.

Junior wide receiver Keith Nichol had a hunch about what was coming: a fake. After all, Dantonio had used a fake field goal known as "Little Giants" to beat Notre Dame in overtime. "I was hoping he'd call for it," Nichol said. Sure enough, the head Spartan took a chance with a fake punt he had dubbed "Mousetrap." Why "Mousetrap?" "We had to get them to take the cheese," Dantonio explained with a big grin after the game.

It didn't start well. The Spartans took a delay of game penalty when freshman receiver Bennie Fowler lined up on the wrong side. The team had always practiced "Mousetrap" to be run along their own sideline, but this time the ball was on the far hash.

The Wildcats took the bait and went for the cheese. Fowler slid behind the defense, and punter Aaron Bates hit him with a first-down pass. Unlike the Notre Dame game, taking a chance didn't win the game. It did, however, turn all the momentum State's way. The Spartans scored on the next play, followed that up with an 88-yard touchdown drive, and went on to win 35-27.

Our lives are the sum total of the chances we have taken — or have not taken — along the way. Every decision we make every day involves taking a chance. Maybe it will work out for the better; maybe it won't. We won't know unless we take a chance.

On the other hand, our regrets often center on the chances we pass by. The missed chance that has the most destructive and devastating effect on our lives comes when we fail to follow Jesus. He calls us all to surrender to him, to commit to him exactly as he called Simon, Andrew, James, and John.

What they did is unsettling. Without hesitation, without telling Jesus to give them time to think about it or wrap up the loose ends of their lives or tell all their friends good-bye, they walked away from a productive living and from their families. They took a chance on this itinerant preacher.

So must we. What have we got to lose? Nothing worthwhile. What have we got to gain? Everlasting life with God. If that's not worth taking a chance on, nothing is.

To have a special season, you have to be willing to roll the dice at times.
— Quarterback Kirk Cousins on taking chances

To take a chance and surrender our lives to Jesus is
to trade hopelessness and death for hope and life.

THE HEALING TOUCH

Read Matthew 17:14-20.

"If you have faith as small as a mustard seed, you can say to this mountain, 'Move from here to there' and it will move. Nothing will be impossible for you" (v. 20).

The Trice family prayed, and the perplexing brain condition that had debilitated their son disappeared.

The culmination of guard Travis Trice's basketball career at MSU came in his senior season of 2014-15. Head coach Tom Izzo made the risky move of turning the team over to a player who until then had averaged only 22 minutes per game because of various injuries.

Trice rewarded his coach's faith by leading the team in scoring and assists. He was the team's MVP. On March 29, 2015, in the finals of the NCAA Tournament's Elite Eight, he scored 15 points and handed out five assists. MSU beat Louisville in overtime and was on its way to the Final Four. Trice was named the MVP of the regional finals.

It had never come easy for him. He was "a skinny, undersized guard who received no big-time recruiting love until right before his senior season." Except from Izzo, "a man who can appreciate the perils of being a little man, and who likes a kid with spunk."

The iconic head coach stuck with Trice even through the horrible time when "a frightening and still undiagnosed [brain] condition in 2012 left him sapped of strength." Trice didn't tell his family for weeks as the doctors could find no explanation for his symptoms. He couldn't find the strength to get out of bed and was losing weight rapidly.

When Travis finally told his family, mom and dad Trice knew what to do. They headed straight to church and launched a time of earnest prayer. His condition cleared up almost immediately, resulting in a turnaround in his personal life as his faith deepened.

If we believe in miraculous healing at all, we have pretty much come to consider it to be a relatively rare occurrence. When we encounter a need for healing in our lives, our response is to turn immediately to the world. This is okay; God gave doctors and medical science the knowledge and the ability to help us. But we must also turn to the greatest healer of them all by making prayer a necessary part of the process as the Trice family did.

The truth is that divine healing occurs with quite astonishing regularity; the problem is our perspective. We are usually quite effusive in our thanks to and praise for a doctor or a particular medicine without considering that God is the one who is responsible for all healing.

We should remember that "natural" healing occurs because our bodies react as God created them to. Every time we get over a cold or recover from a wound or a cut: Those healings are divine; they are miraculous. Faith healing is really nothing more — or less — than giving credit where credit is due.

As strangely as [Trice's] condition began, it disappeared, and Travis almost immediately became a man of deep faith.
— ESPN *writer Dana O'Neil on the results of the Trice family's prayer*

God does in fact heal continuously everywhere; all too often we just don't notice.

DAY 86

STRANGE BUT TRUE

Read Isaiah 55.

"My thoughts are not your thoughts, neither are your ways my way" (v. 8).

From our contemporary perspective, one word most adequately describes much about the early days of athletics at what would become Michigan State University: strange.

For instance, the first athletic equipment at Michigan Agricultural College consisted of a trapeze and some swinging rings hung from campus trees. A Saturday in the fall of 1873 featured a big sporting event on campus: a match hunt between the sophomores and the juniors. They bagged 79 squirrels, twelve pigeons, nine quail, four turkeys, six partridges, and eight ducks.

Historically, the university's most successful sport is men's cross country, which has won eight national championships. The students started the whole thing on their own with an intramural run in 1907. On April 13, a meet was held between two teams drawn from the student body.

Football officially began in 1896, but earlier attempts to field a team were made. A squad in 1884 didn't play any games for reasons that have been lost in time; they did have their picture taken. The same is true for a team in 1888, which also didn't play any games and "may have been organized for the express purpose of having its picture taken."

Basketball was played in the old Armory Building from 1899

until 1918. The backboards were attached flush to brick walls. Overhead girders were so low that Aggie shooters became proficient at lofting long shots over them. They also became accomplished at making layups by springing up on a wooden ledge that encircled the court. The basketball team played its games in Demonstration Hall from 1930-40, sharing the facility with the ROTC unit and its horse cavalry section that played indoor polo.

Those early days of Spartan sports were just strange.

Many things in life are so strange their existence can't really be explained. How else can we account for the sport of curling, tofu, or that people go to bars hoping to meet the "right" person? Isn't it strange that someone would hear the life-changing message of salvation in Jesus Christ and then walk away from it?

And how strange is that plan of salvation that God has for us? Just consider what God did. He could have come roaring down, annihilating everyone whose sinfulness offended him, which, of course, is pretty much all of us. Then he could have brushed off his hands, nodded the divine head, and left a scorched planet in his wake. All in a day's work.

Instead, God came up with a totally novel plan: He would save the world by becoming a human being, letting himself be humiliated, tortured, and killed, thus establishing a kingdom of justice and righteousness that will last forever.

In 1871, a MAC baseball team traveled to Detroit to play a game. [It was] rained out and Aggie players [had to] hitch-hike home.
— Spartan Saga *on the strange beginnings of MSU baseball*

**It's strange but true: God allowed himself
to be killed on a cross to save the world.**

AS A RULE

Read Luke 5:27-32.

"Why do you eat and drink with tax collectors and 'sinners'?" (v. 30b)

Before the 1965 season began, State head football coach Duffy Daugherty served notice he was going to break one of the college game's longstanding unwritten rules.

Others may have missed it, but Charles "Bubba" Smith knew exactly what it meant that day Daugherty named his starting defense. Smith, of course, is a Spartan legend. He twice earned All-American honors as a defensive end (1965 and '66), is one of only three players to have his jersey number retired by the program (Don Coleman and George Webster are the other two.), and was inducted into the College Football Hall of Fame in 1988.

In that pre-season team meeting, Daugherty called out eleven names and their positions. The defensive starters included tackle Harold Lucas, safety Jess Phillips, Smith, back Jim Summers, linebacker Charlie Thornhill, and Webster a roverback.

That meant six African-Americans would be starting on one defense at a time when Southern teams were all white. Even colleges that had integrated obeyed one of college football's most ironclad unwritten rules: Don't recruit too many African-Americans and, for goodness sake, don't play too many of them. To do so was to risk losing alumni money and fan support.

"You just didn't do it," said Clinton Jones, the star halfback of the 1965 and '66 teams. Daugherty took a real chance in that with ten starters on offense and defense, his program would either reject or reinforce that unwritten racist rule.

He understood the significance of his decision. He knew, too, that times were changing, and so he purposefully decided to step out ahead of them. The rule-breaking Spartans of 1965 and '66 went 19-1-1 and won back-to-back Big Ten and national titles.

You live by rules that others set up. Some lender determined the interest rate on your mortgage and your car loan. You work hours and shifts somebody else established. Someone else decided what school district your house sits in.

Jesus encountered societal rules also. These included a strict set of religious edicts that dictated what company he should keep, what people, in other words, were fit for him to socialize with, talk to, or share a meal with. Jesus simply ignored the rules. He chose love instead of mindless obedience, and he demonstrated his disdain for society's rules by mingling with the outcasts, the lowlifes, the poor, and the misfits.

You, too, have to choose when you find yourself in the presence of someone whom society disparages or your peers declare to be undesirable. Will you choose the rules or will you choose love?

Are you willing to be a rebel for love — as Jesus was for you?

Duffy [Daugherty] took a chance, [and] I appreciate what he did for me and the other black players.
— All-Big Ten linebacker Charlie Thornhill

Society's rules dictate who is acceptable
and who is not, but love in the name of Jesus
knows no such distinctions.

DAY 88

ULTIMATE MAKEOVER

Read 2 Corinthians 5:11-21.

"If anyone is in Christ, he is a new creation; the old has gone, the new has come!" (v. 17)

One of Michigan State's greatest football players presented one of three faces to those around him, making himself over as circumstances dictated.

The side of Javon Ringer with which most State fans are familiar is the football star. From 2005-08, Ringer rushed for 4,389 yards, second in Spartan history to Lorenzo White. As a senior, he led the nation in scoring, carries, and rushing touchdowns. His 22 touchdowns that season still constitute the MSU record (tied by Jeremy Langford in 2014). He was a consensus All-America.

But there was more to Ringer than the high flying athlete on the football field. "Hidden beneath his fierce running style [lay] a little boy at heart." He watched cartoons on Saturday mornings and liked to sneak up behind anyone who happened to be nearby and startle them. He was a daydreamer who always needed a cup of coffee at position meetings. He was so gullible he fell for it when other running backs sent him to see the coaches though he hadn't been summoned at all. Players would often usher him onto the practice field when his name hadn't been called.

But there was yet a third side to Ringer: that of the adult. He was and is a committed Christian who at State demonstrated the "maturity and loyalty of a man three times his age." He unfailingly diverted all the credit for his success to his blockers. Off the field, he "never met an autograph he [wouldn't] sign, a picture he [wouldn't] take or a smile he couldn't make." He was often the first MSU athlete to volunteer his time for community services ranging from speaking to younger students, attending charity fundraisers, or working a booth at an elementary school carnival.

There was just much more to Javon Ringer than met the eye.

Ever considered a makeover? TV shows show us how changes in clothes, hair, and makeup and some weight loss can radically alter the way a person looks. But these changes are only skin deep unlike the makeover Javon Ringer routinely made according to what was needed of him. Even with a makeover, the real you — the person inside — remains unchanged. How can you make over that part of you?

By giving your heart and soul to Jesus — just as you give up your hair to the makeover stylist. You won't look any different; you won't dance any better; you won't suddenly start talking smarter. The change is on the inside where you are brand new because the model for all you think and feel is now Jesus. He is the one you care about pleasing. Made over by Jesus, you realize that gaining his good opinion — not the world's — is all that really matters. And he isn't the least interested in how you look but how you act.

For the adult [Javon Ringer], it's about providing for family and honoring God.
                    — Sportswriter Jacob Carpenter

**Jesus is the ultimate makeover artist; he can make
you over without changing the way you look.**

A LONG SHOT

Read Matthew 9:9-13.

"[Jesus] saw a man named Matthew sitting at the tax collector's booth. 'Follow me,' he told him, and Matthew got up and followed him" (v. 9).

He didn't play high school ball and wound up in the military. Yet this long shot became "the greatest non-recruit in college basketball history."

Johnny Green was so short that he never tried out for his high school basketball team. After he graduated, he worked a while and then joined the Army. He was in Japan when he turned 20 and something surprising happened: He sprouted to 6-foot-5.

Green tried out for and made the base basketball team. Dick Evans, the base football coach, noticed him and was impressed by his jumping ability. Evans had played at State under Biggie Munn, so he wrote MSU basketball coach Forddy Anderson. On leave in October 1955, Green visited the Michigan State campus. Anderson told him to come back when he got out of the service.

Green did just that. He enrolled in school and walked into the coach's office and said, "Here I am." Anderson didn't remember this would-be walk-on and told him to go practice with the freshman team, figuring he'd never see him again.

Green was a poor shot, but when assistant coach Bob Stevens suggested he try rebounding the ball, Green soared above the rim and snagged every shot. Excited, Stevens ran and told Anderson to come with him. They found Green on one of the three courts, consistently jumping up and hanging from a 12-foot cable. He "is the difference between nothing and winning the Big Ten championship," Anderson said before Green ever played a game.

Green was 23 when he played his first varsity game in January 1957. He led the Spartans to two Big Ten titles and earned All-Big Ten honors three times. He was the league MVP in 1958-59 and was first-team All-America. State's annual rebounding award is named in his honor. His jersey number 24 has been retired.

Like Johnny Green, Matthew the tax collector was a long shot. In his case, he was an unlikely person to be a confidant of the Son of God. While we may not get all warm and fuzzy about the IRS, our government's revenue agents are nothing like Matthew and his ilk. He bought a franchise, paying the Roman Empire for the privilege of extorting, bullying, and stealing everything he could from his own people. Tax collectors of the time were "despicable, vile, unprincipled scoundrels."

And yet, Jesus said only two words to this lowlife: "Follow me." Jesus knew that this long shot would make an excellent disciple.

It's the same with us. While we may not be quite as vile as Matthew was, none of us can stand before God with our hands clean and our hearts pure. We are all impossibly long shots to enter God's Heaven. That is, until we do what Matthew did: get up and follow Jesus.

Find out what this guy needs and get it to him, no matter what.
 — *Forddy Anderson when he saw long-shot Johnny Green rebound*

**Jesus changes us from being long shots
to enter God's Kingdom to being sure things.**

I DOUBT IT!

Read John 20:24-29.

"Stop doubting and believe" (v. 27c).

The Spartan players and coaches said they never doubted they would win the 2015 Cotton Bowl. In all honesty, for much of the game they constituted a distinct minority.

As the fourth quarter rolled along, Baylor led 41-21. The Bears' offense had simply shredded the proud Spartan defense for three quarters. Any notion of a comeback seemed farfetched.

"You know it was funny," said senior safety Kurtis Drummond. Despite the situation, "You just kind of felt the vibe around the team remain positive. [W]e just never let ourselves get down." In other words, the players never doubted they could still win.

And they did, scoring 21 unanswered points in the fourth quarter to pull off the biggest bowl comeback in school history.

A 50-yard pass play from Connor Cook to senior wide receiver Keith Mumphery set up an 8-yard touchdown pass to tight end Josiah Price. The score made it 41-28 with 12:09 remaining. Cook then led the Spartans on a 61-yard drive with senior running back Jeremy Langford crashing over from the 1. With 4:55 left, State trailed only 41-35.

MSUs beleaguered defense had to make a stand to give the offense a chance. It did, forcing a 43-yard field-goal try with 65 seconds left. End Marcus Rush, who set a school record with his 53 starts, crashed through to block the kick. Safety R.J. Williamson scooped the ball up and returned it to the Baylor 45, "triggering a Green and White frenzy" among the believers in the stadium.

With 17 seconds left, Cook completed the comeback that many doubted could ever happen by finding Mumphery for a 10-yard touchdown pass. State had an improbable 42-41 win.

Head coach Mark Dantonio had a simple, yet powerful explanation for his team's win: "We had a belief that we could come back." The Spartans never doubted.

Doubt is intrinsic to the Christian faith. Even the most faithful and steadfast of us inevitably have moments in which we wonder. Maybe we doubt that we are spiritual enough. Maybe we doubt there really is a resurrection. If only we could see Jesus face-to-face as Thomas did, he who doubted; that would remove all doubt.

Spiritual doubt takes two forms: questioning our faith and total faithlessness. The latter, of course, is inexpressibly dangerous, but doubt doesn't inevitably lead us away from our faith.

On the contrary, doubt can be healthy if it does not send us into a spiral of guilt that paralyzes us spiritually. Doubt is constructive if it spurs us to pursue answers through greater study, more intense prayer, and a conscious seeking to draw closer to Jesus. Doubt can then serve as the impetus to stronger faith

Since our faith is in things unseen, the antidote to doubt is always found in belief. We are subject to the same command that Jesus gave Thomas: "Stop doubting and believe."

I never lost belief. I never doubted myself or our team.
— Connor Cook on the 2015 Cotton Bowl

When doubt creeps into our faith life, we must resolutely 'Stop doubting and believe.'

RAISING A STINK

Read John 11:1-16, 38-44.

"'But, Lord,' said Martha, the sister of the dead man, 'by this time there is a bad odor, for he has been there four days.' Then Jesus said, 'Did I not tell you that if you believed, you would see the glory of God?'" (vv. 39-40)

In Biggie Munn's first game as State's head football coach, his team stunk the place up both literally and figuratively.

That first game was Sept. 27, 1947. Munn had spent eight years as Michigan's line coach, and his old boss, Fritz Crisler, wasn't too happy about his taking the job at State. Munn was convinced Crisler would do all he could to embarrass him. He did. Crisler kept his starters in for the full 60 minutes as Michigan crushed Michigan State 55-0.

So the Spartans dropped a figurative bomb in Munn's debut: a stinkbomb. They literally didn't smell like a bunch of fresh roses before and during the game either.

As the team prepared to dress for the game, raw sewage began to flood the visitor's locker room. It stopped only after some four inches of filth covered the floor. The players dressed standing on benches, "balancing themselves carefully while trying to ignore the overpowering stench." Once the players had their cleats on, they "leaped off the bench and splashed toward the door and dry safety." They arrived on the sideline with sewage dripping off their legs and shoes.

Munn and his players were convinced Michigan flooded the dressing room on purpose. Informed of the situation, officials simply shrugged it off and said a pipe must have cracked.

The incident provided Munn with an outlet for his rage about the game. He was so downcast he didn't even want to see his players after the awful defeat. But he realized he could use the flooding to help them focus on something else and forget the loss. He went on a rampage, raging with tears in his eyes about Michigan's unleashing the sewage into the dressing room.

We live in a smelly world. Sewage, full garbage cans on a summer day, dirty sneakers, rotten meat — they stink. We also live in an aromatic world. Roses, coffee percolating, freshly laundered clothes, your loved one's body spray — they intoxicate.

Nothing, however, stinks both literally and metaphorically as does death. Literally: Think road kill. Metaphorically: Think life's end. We get both in the account of Jesus' raising of Lazarus from the dead. It's a tableau right out of a Christian-themed horror house with Martha's concern about the smell and the image of Lazarus stumbling out of the grave wrapped in his burial cloths.

But it's a glorious story that soars far beyond a trite Halloween scenario. In it, Jesus reveals himself to be the Lord of death as well as life. Death no longer stinks to high heaven but instead becomes the pathway to high heaven. Under Jesus' dominion, death itself becomes a sweet fragrance indeed.

We didn't think it was accidental, let's put it that way.
— Star halfback George Guerre on the locker room flooding in 1947

Because of Jesus, rather than stinking to high heaven, death is the way to high heaven.

GOOD LUCK

Read Acts 1:15-25.

"Then they prayed, 'Lord, you know everyone's heart. Show us which of these two you have chosen.' . . . Then they cast lots" (vv. 24, 25a).

One writer called it luck. Whatever it was, two fumble recoveries in less than a minute propelled the Spartans to a bowl win.

On Dec. 29, 2012, State met TCU in the Buffalo Wild Wings Bowl in Tempe, Ariz. The game turned out as expected in that defenses dominated. Both units had the top-rated defenses in their respective conferences. Especially did yards come at a premium for the Spartans; they managed what was described as "an anemic 227" of them all night. Thus, with little chance of an offensive explosion in the last half, the Spartans were in real trouble when they fell behind 13-0 at halftime.

But redshirt freshman quarterback Connor Cook provided some spark for the struggling offense in the third quarter. He led the team on the longest touchdown drive in State's bowl history. It covered 90 yards, took 14 plays, and ended with a 15-yard scoring toss to freshman Aaron Burbridge, who would be the Big Ten's Wide Receiver of the Year his senior season.

The "luck" came between the seven- and eight- minute marks of the fourth quarter. Quarterback Andrew Maxwell was crushed and fumbled at the MSU 36, but tackle Skyler Burkland fell on the ball. Thus did the recovery prevent a makeable field goal that

SPARTANS

would have given the Frogs a 16-7 lead and a virtual lock.

State punted on the next play, and Mike Sadler boomed a 55-yard kick. The Frog receiver muffed it and State recovered at the TCU 4. Le'Veon Bell got the touchdown and a 14-13 lead.

Senior Dan Conroy's 47-yard field goal with 1:01 left provided the difference in the 17-16 win that may not have happened but for "a little bit of fumbles luck."

Do you ever seriously think sometimes that other people have all the luck? Some guy wins a lottery while you can't get a raise of a few lousy bucks at work. The football takes a lucky bounce the other team's way and the Spartans lose a game. If you have any luck to speak of, it's bad.

To ascribe anything that happens in life to blind luck, however, is to believe that random chance controls everything, including you. But here's the truth: Luck exists only as a makeshift explanation for something beyond our ken. Even when the apostles in effect flipped a coin to pick the new guy, they acknowledged that the lots revealed to them a decision God had already made.

It's true that we can't explain why some people skate merrily through life while others suffer in horrifying ways. We don't know why good things happen to bad people and vice versa. But none of it results from luck, unless, as the disciples did, you want to attribute that name to the force that does indeed control the universe; you know — the one more commonly called God.

It won [State] the game.
— Writer Bill Connelly on the 'little bit of fumbles luck'

**A force does exist that is in charge of your life,
but it isn't luck; it's God.**

ON CALL

Read 1 Samuel 3:1-18.

"The Lord came and stood there, calling as at the other times, 'Samuel! Samuel!' Then Samuel said, 'Speak, for your servant is listening'" (v. 10).

Michigan State's title hopes were right out there on the floor, writhing in pain. Then head coach Tim Izzo issued a call to war.

In the 2000 championship finals against Florida, MSU faced some real challenges from the Gators' all-court pressure and endless bench. "We can beat this," Izzo told his assistants in speaking of the press. The key was getting the ball to point guard Mateen Cleaves, the program's only three-time All-America.

The Spartans did just that. Forward A.J. Granger inbounded the ball to Big-Ten Player of the year Morris Peterson or guard Charlie Bell, who got the ball to Cleaves, who then bolted up the middle of the floor. Not once in the first half did State lose the ball in the backcourt. With four minutes left in the half, Florida simply gave up and quit pressing. MSU led 43-32 at halftime.

After the break, though, the Gators cut the lead to six with 16:18 to play. That's when a Florida player collided with Cleaves, who "wound up in a grimacing heap by the baseline" with an ankle injury. Izzo checked on Cleaves and then returned to his somewhat shellshocked team. "We're going to war!" he shouted. "They took out our leader. Who's going to step up?"

The whole team answered Izzo's call. Bell moved to the point, and reserve guard Mike Chappell stepped up and scored five quick points to stifle the Florida rally. Cleaves was in the locker room for 4 1/2 minutes of game action, and during that time, the fired-up Spartans actually extended their lead.

Cleaves did return, "hobbling about for the final 12 minutes by the grace of ice, tape and a brace." But as *Sports Illustrated* writer Alexander Wolff put it, the star's return to the game "was mere stagecraft. Florida was already broken."

State won the national championship 89-76.

A team player is someone who does whatever the coach calls upon him to do for the good of the team. Something quite similar occurs when God places a specific call upon a Christian's life.

This is much scarier, though, than responding when a star player is injured as the Spartans did against Florida. The way many folks understand it is that answering God's call means going into the ministry, packing the family up, and moving halfway around the world to some place where folks have never heard of air conditioning, fried chicken, cell phones, or the Spartans. Zambia. The Philippines. Some place in the Orient.

Not for you, no thank you. And who can blame you?

But God usually calls folks to serve him where they are. In fact, God put you where you are right now, and he has a purpose in placing you there. Wherever you are, you are called to serve him.

I dropped a couple of tears, but I told the trainer he'd have to amputate my leg to keep me out of this one.
— Mateen Cleaves on answering the call and getting back in the game

God calls you to serve him right now
right where he has put you, wherever that is.

DAY 94

HERO WORSHIP

Read 1 Samuel 16:1-13.

"Do not consider his appearance or his height, for . . . the Lord does not look at the things man looks at. . . . The Lord looks at the heart" (v. 7).

They weren't heroes just because they pulled off "the most glorious achievement in Michigan State athletic history" to that time. They were heroes also because they saved lives during a hotel fire.

They were the football Spartans of 1953, who won the Big Ten and landed in the Rose Bowl.

By all accounts, the team had a grand old time in California. At a movie studio, they hobnobbed with movie stars like Doris Day. At the Big Ten club dinner, halfback Billy Wells sat with Debbie Reynolds; they then went on a date, hitting some night spots.

The squad was so small that a *Los Angeles Times* sportswriter called them "midgets." Nevertheless, they pulled off a heroic effort in the Rose Bowl, overcoming a 14-0 deficit to upset the heavily favored Bruins 28-20. Wells was named the game's MVP.

But the Spartans had established themselves as heroes even before the game. Various team members were lounging around their hotel pool on Sunday, Dec. 20, when thick black smoke began pouring from a fourth-floor window. The players reacted immediately and heroically.

Center Joe Badaczewski and fullback Evan Slonac were among the players who rushed up the stairs to grab a fire hose and pour

SPARTANS

water on the flames "while red hot pieces of paint and plaster were falling on and around them." Other players relayed cold, wet towels to them to cover their heads. They had the fire under control before the hook and ladder trucks arrived.

End Bill Quinlan and tackle Hank Bullough moved through the hotel alerting tenants. At one room, they smashed a locked door down and discovered an elderly invalid in a wheelchair. The duo carried the woman down four flights of stairs to safety.

A hero is commonly thought of as someone who performs brave and dangerous feats that save or protect someone's life as the Spartans did at the Rose Bowl. You figure that excludes you.

But ask your son about that when you show him how to bait a hook or throw a football, or your daughter when you show up for her softball game or her honors night at school. Look into the eyes of those Little Leaguers you help coach.

Ask God about heroism when you're steady in your faith. For God, a hero is a person with the heart of a servant. And if a hero is a servant who acts to save other's lives, then the greatest hero of all is Jesus Christ.

God seeks heroes today, those who will proclaim the name of their hero — Jesus — proudly and boldly, no matter how others may scoff or ridicule. God knows heroes when he sees them — by what's in their hearts.

These young men prevented a major fire, one that could have caused great loss of life and property.
— TV sports director Bob Shackleton on the Spartan heroes

**God's heroes are those who remain steady
in their faith while serving others.**

THE END

Read Revelation 22:1-17.

"I am the Alpha and the Omega, the First and the Last, the Beginning and the End" (v. 13).

Duffy Daugherty's Hall-of-Fame coaching career ended with a mediocre season, but his team gave him one last hurrah: an upset of an undefeated Ohio State team.

The Spartans of 1972 finished with an underwhelming 5-5-1 record. When the team slipped to 2-4-1, Daugherty announced the night before the Purdue game that he would retire at the end of what was his 19th season as the head Spartan.

The '72 squad incredibly had 11 All-Big Ten honorees and ten NFL draft picks but was doomed by its offense. They couldn't score, averaging only 14.4 points a game, 105th in the nation out of 127 teams. They were shut out twice and scored only six points in two other games and ten points in another game.

After Daugherty's announcement of his retirement, the team responded with a 22-12 defeat of Purdue. Next up was 5th-ranked Ohio State, not surprisingly a heavy favorite.

But the Spartans churned out 334 yards rushing and used a league-record four field goals from Dutch kicker Dirk Krijt to pull off a 19-12 upset.

The game-winning touchdown came on a 6-yard run in the third quarter by quarterback Mark Niesen. He was a safety who earned some All-American mentions in 1971, but after the 1-2 start in '72, Daugherty sat down next to him on the bench. "How would you like to play quarterback next week?" he asked. "Well, I don't think I could do any worse," Niesen responded.

When he scored his touchdown against the Buckeyes, Niesen threw the ball into the air. An official came to him and said, "Son, next time you hand that ball to me!" Niesen started laughing and said, "If there is a next time, I promise I will."

In their locker room, the excited Spartans presented game balls to their head coach and to Krijt.

Duffy Daugherty's career at Michigan State is another example of one of life's basic truths: Everything ends. Even the stars have a life cycle, though admittedly it's rather lengthy. Erosion eventually will wear a boulder to a pebble. Life itself is temporary; all living things have a beginning and an end.

Within the framework of our own lifetimes, we experience endings. Loved ones, friends, and pets die; relationships fracture; jobs dry up; our health, clothes, lawn mowers, TV sets — they all wear out. Even this world as we know it will end.

But one of the greatest ironies of God's gift of life is that not even death is immune from the great truth of creation that all things must end. That's because through Jesus' life, death, and resurrection, God himself acted to end any power death once had over life.

Because of Jesus, the end of life has ended. God's eternity — which is outside time and has no end — is ours for the claiming.

This has to rate very high on my list.
    — Duffy Daugherty in 1972 after his last defeat of Ohio State

Everything ends; thanks to Jesus, so does death.

THE END   191

NOTES
(by Devotion Day Number)

1   they believed all competitive . . . work as healthful exercise.": Fred W. Stabley, *The Spartans* (Tomball, Texas: Strode Publishers, 2nd Ed., 1988), p. 13.

1   the school faculty launched an effort to abolish football.: Stabley, *The Spartans*, p. 13.

1   Joining in the effort to . . . leadership in chapel each morning.: Stabley, *The Spartans*, p. 14.

1   If we must have football, I want the kind that wins.: Stabley, *The Spartans* p. 14.

2   "as one of the starting running backs,": "Gerald Holmes," *MSUSpartans.com*, www.msu spartans.com/sports/m-footbl/mtt/gerald_holmes_855512.html.

2   "It was tough," . . . kind of hit me.": Chris Solari, "MSU's Gerald Holmes Overcomes Loss of Grandmother," *Lansing State Journal*, Sept. 18, 2016, http://www.lansingstatejournal.com/story/sports/college/msu/football/2016/09/18/msu-gerald-holmes-overcomes-loss-grand-mother-100-yards-2-tds/90627724/.

2   On Friday, Sept. 17, the day . . . told Holmes to be ready: Solari, "MSU's Gerald Holmes."

2   he followed fullback Prescott . . . open space before him.: Solari, "MSU's Gerald Holmes."

2   It was a tough two weeks. I kept grinding.: Solari, "MSU's Gerald Holmes."

3   Heathcote determined that the . . . direction do the talking.: Lynn Henning, *Spartan Seasons* (Bloomfield Hills, Mich.: Momentum Publishing, 1987), p. 185.

3   As the winter of . . . was pushing Johnson hard.: Henning, *Spartan Seasons*, p. 186.

3   Vincent and Johnson were . . . playing together in college.: Henning, *Spartan Seasons*, p. 186.

3   Assistant coach Vern Payne . . . and nothing more.: Henning, *Spartan Seasons*, p. 187.

3   Forty-eight hours before . . . Johnson in the bag.: Henning, *Spartan Seasons*, pp. 189-90.

3   Alarmed, Payne arranged to . . . entire community and city.: Henning, *Spartan Seasons*, p. 190.

3   After listening to Payne's . . . "I'll sign, Coach.": Henning, *Spartan Seasons*, p. 191.

3   Next fall, I will be attending Michigan State University.: Henning, *Spartan Seasons*, p. 191.

4   Football buffs have called . . . history" of college football.: Stabley, *The Spartans* p. 272.

4   The referee signalled that . . . was the official one.: Stabley, *The Spartans* p. 276.

4   Thirty seconds felt like a . . . an eternity in purgatory.: Chris Solari, "1974 MSU-Ohio State Ending Still Bizarre 40 Years Later," *Lansing State Journal*, Nov. 1, 2014, http://www.lansingstatejournal.com/story/sports/college/msu/football/2014/11/01/msu-ohio-state-ending-still-bizarre-years-later/18352497/.

5   It "kind of snapped my neck back a little bit,": Graham Couch, "Injury at Oregon Altered Amp Campbell's Life," *Lansing State Journal*, Sept. 5, 2014, http://www.lansingstatejournal.com/story/sports/columnists/graham-couch/2014/09/05/injury-oregon-altered-amp-campbells-life/15109817/.

5   A burning sensation ran through . . . had fractured two vertebrae.: Adam Biggers, "Amp Campbell Will Always Be a Michigan State Spartan," *BleacherReport.com*, Aug. 22, 2010, http://bleacherreport.com/articles/441193-amp-campbell-will-always-be-a-michigan-state-spartan#.

5   He underwent spinal-fusion . . . win this one for Amp,": B.J. Schecter, "Turning the Corner," *SI.com*, Sept. 13, 1999, http://www.si.com/vault/1999/09/13/8110447/turning-the-corner.

5   "The chances of coming back . . . finish his senior season.": Biggers, "Amp Campbell Will Always Be a Michigan State Spartan."

5   It is an amazing comeback story.: Couch, "Injury at Oregon ."

6   Writer Jeremy Warnemuende declared . . . 2010 league title coming: Jeremy Warnemuende, "At Long Last," in *Reaching Higher: Mark Dantonio and the Rise of Michigan State Football* (Chicago: Triumph Books LLC, 2016), p. 54.

6   "Our goal was to win the championship. That's our No. 1 goal,": Michigan State Earns Share of Big Ten Title," *ESPN.com*, Nov. 28, 2010, http://www.espn.com/ncf/recap/_/id/303310213.

6   "We could've ended it . . . but we'll take it,": "Michigan State Earns Share."

6   We can't do it the easy way, can we?: Warnemuende, "At Long Last," in *Reaching Higher*, p. 54.

7   "The season on the line, . . . a touchdown all night.": "No. 5 Michigan State Wins Big Ten Championship," *BigTen.org*, Dec. 5, 2015, http://www.bigten.org/sports/m-footbl/recaps/120515aaa.html.

7   "I was just trying to make a big play for my brothers.": "No. 5 Michigan State Wins."

7   On a play that eventually took six interminable seconds,: "No. 5 Michigan State Wins."
7   six Iowa defenders ganged . . . and pushed him backward.: "No. 5 Michigan State Wins."
8   Michigan's coaches and the ABC . . . before the play was over.: "2001 Michigan vs. Michigan State Football Game," *Wikipedia, the free encylopedia*, https://en.wikipedia.org/wiki/2001_Michigan_vs_Michigan_State_football_game.
8   The Wolverine radio announcer . . . to pray for forgiveness.": Gillian Van Stratt, "Michigan Versus Michigan State: Memorable Moments," *Mlive.com*, Nov. 1, 2013, http://www.mlive.com/sports/index.ssf/2013/11/michigan_versus_michigan_state.html.
8   That play, as much as . . . prove that timer wrong.: "2001 Michigan vs. Michigan State," *Wikipedia, the free encyclopedia.*
9   On July 31 before his senior . . . going to be all right.: Brian Calloway, "Michigan State Player Helps Save Teenager's Life," *USA Today*, Aug. 5, 2013, http://www.usatoday.com/story/sports/ncaaf/bigten/2013/08/05/michigan-state-micajah-reynolds-helps-save-teenagers-life/2621903/.
9   "I felt like I was . . . keep going. You got it.": Adam Rittenberg, "Spartans' Reynolds Helps Save Teen's Life," *ESPN.com*, Aug. 6, 2013, http://www.espn.com/blog/bigten/post/_/id/80880/spartans-reynolds-helps-save-teens-life.
9   "Life is so delicate, . . . everything that you're given.": Calloway, "Michigan State Player."
9   I've still got my . . . drenched in his blood.: Calloway, "Michigan State Player."
10 the college sponsored a contest . . . informed him of the error.: "Traditions: The Nickname," *MSUSpartans.com*, http://www.msuspartans.com/trads/msu-traditions.html.
10 No [one[called up the . . . experiment, the name took.: "Traditions: The Nickname."
11 In January 2001, assistant hockey . . . would be "a nifty event.": Lynn Henning, *Spartan Seasons II* (Bloomfield Hills, Mich.: Sports Seasons Publishing, 2006), p. 358.
11 hockey had been one of . . . deep and devoted fan base.: Henning, *Spartan Seasons II*, p. 357.
11 McAuliffe's suggestion was . . . was dubbed the Cold War.: Henning, *Spartan Seasons II*, p. 358.
11 Hours after the ducats . . . watch a hockey game.: Henning, *Spartan Seasons II*, pp. 358-59.
11 a temporary rink was . . . arrived in time.: Henning, *Spartan Seasons II*, p. 359.
11 Pulling off an outdoor . . . Hollywood-grade production.: Henning, *Spartan Seasons II*, p. 359.
12 In the 1940s, the students . . . someone's vivid imagination.: Robert Bao, "The MSU Songs: Smashing Through the Myths," *Michigan State University Alumni Magazine*, Aug. 26, 2013, alumni.msu.edu/newsarticle.cfmid=573.
12 All kinds of claims . . . were thrown around.: Bao, "The MSU Songs."
13 "am absolute beast,": Adam Rittenberg, "Spartans Rally to Stun Wisconsin in OT," *ESPN.com*, Oct. 27, 2012, http://www.espn.com/blog/bigten/post/_/id/63382/spartans-rally-to-stun-wisconsin-in-ot.
13 "Badgers would escape with an ugly [10-3] win.": Rittenberg, "Spartans Rally."
13 "a seemingly blanketed Bennie Fowler": Rittenberg, "Spartans Rally."
13 He let loose with a . . . accompanied his boogie moves.: Brian Bennett, "Wisconsin Win Had Dantonio Dancing," *ESPN.com*, Oct. 30, 2012, http://www. espn.com/blog/bigten/post/_/id/63796/wisconsin-win-had-dantonio-dancing.
13 Everybody was just . . . beat 'em, join 'em, so . . . .": Bennett, "Wisconsin Win."
14 "isn't likely to produce a big winning season.": Stabley, *The Spartans*, p. 170.
14 "not much was expected . . . Duffy's chronic optimism.: Stabley, *The Spartans*, p. 170.
14 "hurtled [its] way to glory.": Stabley, *The Spartans*, p. 173.
14 The athletic department waived . . . against the nearest radio.: Stabley, *The Spartans,* p. 175.
14 State appears to be at . . . a top-flight outfit.: Stabley, *The Spartans*, pp. 170-71.
15 he was described as ranting . . . described as "free spirited.": Fred Stabley, Jr., and Tim Staudt, *Tales of the Magical Spartans* (Champaign, Ill.: Sports Publishing L.L.C., 2003), p. 63.
15 "Stats . . . don't . . . lie." . . . little smirk on his face.: Stabley, Jr., and Staudt, *Tales of the Magical Spartans*, p. 63.
15 I was kind of a free spirit and was always getting in Jud's doghouse.: Stabley, Jr., and Staudt, *Tales of the Magical Spartans*, p. 63.
16 a player so versatile no one was really sure what position he played.: Joe Rexrode, *Stadium Stories: Michigan State Spartans* (Guilford, Conn.: Globe Pequot Press, 2006), p. 70.
16 Head coach Duffy Daugherty . . . play the whole field.: Rexrode, *Stadium Stories.* p. 76.
16 "George would say, 'Which . . . back to the huddle.": Rexrode, *Stadium Stories*, pp. 77-78.
16 Between the two of us, . . . for the tackle first.: Rexrode, *Stadium Stories*, p. 78.
17 As the clock ticked . . . shock the world!": Rexrode, *Stadium Stories*, p. 153.

17   "the OSU fans were stunned and their heroes were shaken.": Rexrode, *Stadium Stories*, p. 156.

17   "That's when it really . . . starting to get intimidated.": Rexrode, *Stadium Stories*, p. 157.

17   If you see Lee Corso . . . them by beeper number,": Rexrode, *Stadium Stories*, p. 159.

17   For one wondrous evening, . . . very satisfied football prophet.: Rexrode, *Stadium Stories*, p. 159.

18   when he was 19 months . . . underestimated most of his life,": Mark Schlabach, "Kirk Cousins Used to Playing Long Odds," *ESPN.com*, Oct. 21, 2011, http://www.espn.com/college-football/story/_/id/7127370/michigan-state-quarterback-kirk-cousins-used-having-odds-stacked-him.

18   My life has been living evidence of God's ability to do the unexplainable.: Schlabach, "Kirk Cousins Used to Playing Long Odds."

19   As he watched a replay . . . Izzo was furious.: Henning, *Spartan Seasons II*, p. 314.

19   Most galling of all for . . . appalling lack of toughness.: Henning, *Spartan Seasons II*, p. 314.

19   When the players arrived . . . helmets and shoulder pads.: Henning, *Spartan Seasons II*, p. 314.

19   They were then positioned . . . into a blood bath.: Henning, *Spartan Seasons II*, p. 315.

19   When the pads came off, . . . practice of the season.: Henning, *Spartan Seasons II*, p. 315.

19   Breslin Center was about . . . into Spartan Stadium.: Henning, *Spartan Seasons II*, p. 314.

20   They had the boys in . . . did toughen him up some.: Dan Murphy, "Toughness Is a Family Trait," *ESPN.com*, Dec. 30, 2015, http://www.espn.com/blog/bigten/post/_/id/129101/toughness-is-a-family-trait-for-michigan-states-allen-brothers.

20   The Allen brothers set . . . with their toughness.: Murphy, "Toughness Is a Family Trait."

21   "He was a no-brainer over any redshirt freshman.": Rexrode, *Stadium Stories*, p. 165.

21   That decision left the . . . deserved an extended look.: Rexrode, *Stadium Stories*, p. 169.

21   "Drew Stanton Era began with . . . in the second half.: Rexrode, *Stadium Stories*, p. 170.

21   MSU fans chanting his name.: Rexrode, *Stadium Stories*, p. 172.

21   I thought that was great of him.: Rexrode, *Stadium Stories*, p. 170.

22   Van Pelt "was a terror on the football field.": Steve Grinczel, "Brad Van Pelt Was One of MSU's All-Time Greats," *MLive.com*, Feb. 19, 2009, http://www.mlive.com/spartans/index-ssf/2009-02/post_1.html.

22   "an athletic anomaly.": Graham Couch, "MSU's Top 50 Football Players: No. 9 Brad Van Pelt," *Lansing State Journal*, July 30, 2015, http://www.lansingstatejournal.com/story/sports/college/msu/top50-football/2015/07/29/msu-top-50-brad-van-pelt-30842845/.

22   "a mammoth athlete, . . . secondary or returning kicks.": Couch, "MSU's Top 50."

22   "I wished I would have waited,": Grinczel, "Brad Van Pelt."

22   I would've loved to . . . and earn nine letters.: Grinczel, "Brad Van Pelt."

23   "a very good player" who . . . her to be a great player,": Brian Calloway, "Big Heart Fuels Tori Jankoska," *Lansing State Journal*, Feb. 13, 2017, http://www.lansingstatejournal.com/story/sports/college/ms-womens-basketball/2017/02/13/big-heart-fuels-tori-jankoska-record-setting-msu-career/97839780/.

23   She was born with a . . . take her daughter home.: Denise Spann, "Tori Jankoska Rises, Breaks Records," *The State News*, Feb. 27, 2017, http://statenews.com/article/2017/02/tori-jankoska-rises-breaks-records.

23   I didn't know what . . . winner that kid is,": Calloway, "Big Heart Fuels Tori."

23   Her heart is bigger than anything.: Calloway, "Big Heart Fuels Tori."

24   "Something unbelievable happened.": Mark Schlabach, "A Finish for the Ages," *ESPN.com*, Oct. 28, 2015, http://cdn.espn.com/college-football/story/_/page/gamedayfinal/101715/michigan-state-spartans-relish-win.

24   "from total obscurity to . . . gets flipped upside down.": "Michigan State Stuns Michigan with Final-Play Fumble Return," *ESPN.com*, Oct. 17, 2015, http://cdn.espn.com/ncf/recap?gameId=400763542.

24   It can't be true.: Chris Low, "'I'm at a Loss for Words,'" *ESPN.com*, Oct 19, 2015, http://cdn.espn.com/blog/bigten/post/_/id/125417/im-at-a-loss-for-words.

25   "Pro football was George Perles' business, but Michigan State was his passion.": Henning, *Spartan Seasons*, p. 91.

25   his interview turned out to be a mere courtesy.: Henning, *Spartan Seasons*, p. 92

25   Perles became the clear . . . Perles would be named.": Henning, *Spartan Seasons*, p. 94.

25   Perles reacted gracefully . . . it'll come your way.": Henning, *Spartan Seasons*, p. 95.

25   [George] Perles would trade all . . . State as head coach.: Henning, *Spartan Seasons*, p. 91.

26   several of his players . . . "Litwhiler was floored.": Henning, *Spartan Seasons*, p. 243.

26   Among the contraptions he used. . . were flying around the gym.: Henning, *Spartan Seasons*,

![SPARTANS]

SPARTANS

pp. 243-44.

26   It got better when . . . home run at Kobs Field.: Henning, *Spartan Seasons*, p. 244.
26   Boy, he has a good swing.: Henning, *Spartan Seasons*, p. 244.
27   "among the biggest upsets in all college football history": Stabley, *The Spartans*, p. 37.
27   a "very ugly, unacademic structure": Stabley, *The Spartans*, p. 38.
27   "sensed that now the time . . . for work after dark.: Stabley, *The Spartans*, p. 36.
27   "We would be too tired to eat even,": Stabley, *The Spartans*, p. 34.
27   "a phenomenal performance with the fat ball of those days.".: Stabley, *The Spartans*, p. 37.
27   A wild celebration ensued, . . . students returning from Ann Arbor.: Stabley, *The Spartans*, p. 38.
27   No one said so, but . . . of the victory celebration.: Stabley, *The Spartans*, p. 38.
28   As he grew up, Calhoun . . . wind up on his backside.: Zach Schonbrun, "Shilique Calhoun
        Finds a Good Fit," *The New York Times*, Oct. 15, 2015, http://www.nytimes.com/2015/
        10/16/sports/ncaafootball/michigan-state-shilique-calhoun-michigan-college-football.
        html?_r=0.
28   He does what [the coaches] . . . he's a fast learner.: Matt Fortuna, "Calhoun's Dual Role," *ESPN.
        com*, Aug. 29, 2014, http://www.espn.com/blog/bigten/post_/id/106258/calhoun-still-
        improving-on-and-off-the-field.
29   That's when Munn felt . . . down at Oldsmobile.": Stabley, *The Spartans*, p. 141.
29   Apparently he had stepped out of the stands to visit with me.: Stabley, *The Spartans*, p. 141.
30   the "everyman sort of legend". . . the table with the big dogs.": Dana O'Neil, "MSU's Valentine
        Next in Line of Spartan Leaders," *ESPN.com*, Dec. 9, 2015, http://www.espn.com/mens-
        college-basketball/story/_/id/14320710/denzel-valentine-latest-long-line-michigan-state-
        spartan-program-caretakers.
30   Michigan State bequeaths its . . . it remains properly lit.: O'Neil, "MSU's Valentine Next."
31   "walking into a biker bar . . . and sandals with socks.": Ryan McGee, "The Bottom 10," *ESPN.
        com*, Oct. 29, 2014, http://www.espn.com/college-football/story/_/page/bottom102821/
        michigan-wolverines-mess-michigan-state-spartans.
31   "It just felt like we needed . . . them at that point,": Dan Murphy, "MSU Irked by Wolverines'
        Slight," *ESPN.com*, Oct. 25, 2014, http://www.espn.com/college-football/story/_/id/
        11764201/michigan-state-spartans-respond-perceived-slight-michigan-wolverines.
31   The Sunday morning after the . . . calling it "poor sportsmanship.": Brian Bennett, "Brady Hoke
        Apologizes for Stake," *ESPN.com*, Oct. 26, 2014, http://www.espn.com/college-football/
        story/_/id/11767910/brady-hoke-apologizes-michigan-state.
31   They disrespected us right . . . We weren't having that.: Murphy, "MSU Irked."
32   "The Spartans are superior . . . to prove them wrong.": Adam Rittenberg, "Little Brother Takes
        Over the Big House," *ESPN.com*, Oct. 25, 2008, http://www.espn.com/blog/bigten/post/_/
        id/878/little-brother-takes-over-the-big-house.
32   Big Ten Commissioner Jim . . . declared discipline could follow.: "Report: Delany Says Officials
        Mistakenly Awarded TD to Michigan," *ESPN.com*, Oct 27, 2008, http://www.espn.com/
        college-football/news/story?id=3666060.
32   This one counts as . . . culture in this state.: "Spartans Win at Big House," *ESPN.com*, Oct. 25,
        2008, http://www.espn.com/ncf/recap?gameId=282990130.
33   During the last week of . . . just like Freddy Krueger.": Tim Layden, "Altered State," *Sports
        Illustrated*, Oct. 18, 1999, http://www.si.com/vault/1999/10/18/268360/altered state-as-
        michigan-learned-the-hard-way.
33   "and mauled them from . . . were beating them up,": Layden, "Altered State."
33   [Nick] Saban's [nightmare] ploy . . . own Saturday in East Lansing.: Layden, "Altered State."
34   "the best player, that . . . history of MSU's program.": Graham Couch, "MSU's Top 50
        Basketball Players: No. 6 Greg Kelser," *Lansing State Journal*, Sept. 12, 2014, http://www.
        lansingstatejournal.com/story/sports/college/msu/couchonfire/2014/09/12/msu-top-
        50-greg-kelser/15506721/.
34   Payne was such an ace . . . the Michigan State campus.: Stabley and Staudt, *Tales of the Magical
        Spartans*, p. 8.
34   His first visit his senior . . . of the coach's wish list.: Stabley and Staudt, *Tales of the Magical
        Spartans*, p. 9.
34   On signing day, Payne . . . obliged on both accounts.": Stabley and Staudt, *Tales of the
        Magical Spartans*, p. 10.
34   [Greg] Kelser didn't charge [Vern] Payne for the Coke.: Stabley and Staudt,
        Tales of the Magical Spartans, p. 10.

35   As Jack and his dad, . . . sometime during the year.: Adam Rittenberg, "MSU's Conklin Makes Everyone Take Notice," *ESPN.com*, June 16, 2014, http://www.espn.com/blog/bigten/post/_/id/102266/msus-conklin-making-everyone-take-notice.

35   They've looked at him . . . think he's good enough.: Rittenberg, "MSU's Conklin."

36   "She's just our heart and soul.": Graham Hays, "Jefferson Helps Sparty Stomach BGSU," *ESPN.com*, March 20, 2010, http://www.espn.com/ncw/tournament/2010/columns/story?id=5012998&columnist=hays_graham.

36   Her stomach was in such . . . beyond the 2009-10 season.: Hays, "Jefferson Helps Sparty."

36   "It was my night,": Hays, "Jefferson Helps Sparty."

36   I had a little stomach issue, but I had a lot of Mylanta.: Hays, "Jefferson Helps Sparty."

37   While the outcome was disappointing to virtually everyone,": Stabley, *The Spartans*, p. 241.

37   The game of Nov. 19 . . . that late in the season.: Stabley, *The Spartans*, p. 239.

37   ABC declared it had received. . . offer in a Detroit newspaper.: Stabley, *The Spartans*, p. 240.

37   More than 300 writers were . . . ever to work a college game.": Stabley, *The Spartans*, pp. 240-41.

37   The mounting hysteria was incredible.: Stabley, *The Spartans*, p. 239.

38   Head coach John Macklin turned . . . allowed him to stay on.: Steve Grinczel, "Celebrating the Legacy of Gideon Smith," *MSUSpartans.com*, Oct. 15, 2013, www.msuspartans.com/sports/m-football/spec-rel-101513aae.html.

38   the third black man to play . . . "couldn't be printed.": Rexrode, *Stadium Stories*, p. 6.

38   Smith was "a run-stuffing defender": Rexrode, *Stadium Stories*, p. 8.

38   "had the agility of . . . were playing an accordion.": Rexrode, *Stadium Stories*, p. 14.

38   In an age when tackles . . . his speed and power.: Rexrode, *Stadium Stories*, p. 8.

38   The esteem in which . . . the story of so many.: Grinczel, "Celebrating the Legacy."

39   East Lansing found itself . . . was almost humorous.": Henning, *Spartan Seasons*, p. 168.

39   Among the MSU coaches . . . for some soup.: Henning, *Spartan Seasons*, p. 169.

39   After one set of games . . . attack after he had jogged.: Henning, *Spartan Seasons*, p. 170.

39   [John] Benington's death . . . the kind of person he was.: Henning, *Spartan Seasons*, p. 170.

40   The head Wolverine wasn't . . . could to embarrass him.: Rexrode, *Stadium Stories*, p. 36.

40   "I almost broke into tears," . . . room and face my boys.": Rexrode, *Stadium Stories*, p. 39.

40   Disheartened by the loss . . . his players, I'm staying.": Rexrode, *Stadium Stories*, p. 40.

40   I give George Guerre crdit for keeping me in coaching.: Rexrode, *Stadium Stories*, p. 40.

41   When George Perles took . . . give him five seasons: Rexrode, *Stadium Stories*, p. 120.

41   "the most anticipated sporting . . . MSU campus in years.": Rexrode, *Stadium Stories*, p. 132.

41   "the Hoosiers had no chance": Rexrode, *Stadium Stories*, p. 133.

41   The fans kept him . . . for the Heisman Trophy.: Kyle Austin, "Led by Lorenzo White's 56-Carry Day," *Mlive.com*, Oct 17, 2014, http://www.mlive.com/spartans/index.ssf/2014/10/led_by_lorenzo_whites_56_carry.html.

41   The coach once asked . . . you the ball anyway.": Rexrode, *Stadium Stories*, p. 133.

41   The adrenaline was pumping . . . my sleep all night.: Rexrode, *Stadium Stories*, p. 133.

42   The senior reacted to the . . . shocked by the call.: Jeff Kanan, "Fake Field Goal Gives Spartans Overtime Win vs. Notre Dame," in *Reaching Higher*, p. 44.

42   The call caught everyone in the stadium by surprise.: Kanan, "Fake Field Goal Gives Spartans Overtime Win vs. Notre Dame," in *Reaching Heights*, p. 44.

43   "a gangle-armed farmer who hated to diet.": Gary Ronberg, "Delicious Dessert for a Hungry Spartan Crew," *SI.com*, April 3, 1967, http://www.si.com/vault/1967/04/03/608949/delicious-dessert-for-a-hungry-spartan-crew.

43   "the cleverest wrestler I've ever coached.": Ronberg, "Delicious Dessert."

43   "a beautifully proportioned young . . . he finally made weight.": Ronberg, "Delicious Dessert."

43   There wasn't one week . . . worrying about his weight.: Ronberg, "Delicious Dessert."

44   In 1870, Ransom McDonough . . . in parades and at drills.: "First Band Formed in 1870," *SpartanBand.net*, http://spartanband.net/history/origins/.

44   The original members, . . . were all Civil War veterans.: "Traditions: MSU Marching Band," *MSUSpartans.com*, http://www.msuspartans.com/trads/msu-traditions.html.

44   In 1885, a permanent . . . and at public concerts.: "First Band Formed in 1870."

44   For most of its . . . inspections before every performance.: "Traditions: MSU Marching Band."

44   no flutes, clarinets, oboes, or bassoons are used.: "2016 Auditions," *SpartanBand.net*, Jan. 23, 2016, http://spartanband.net/2016-auditions/.

44   these instruments are too . . . large Big Ten stadiums.: "Traditions: MSU Marching Band."

44   Music majors specializing . . . play alto or tenor saxophones: "2016 Auditions."

196

44 Tiny E-flat cornets are . . . the "woodwind-like" parts.: "Traditions: MSU Marching Band."

45 We need you down here.": Adam Rittenberg, "Spartans Feeling Rosy After Taking Final Step," *ESPN.com*, Dec. 8, 2013, http://www.espn.com/blog/bigten/post/_/id/91192/spartans-feeling-rosy-after-taking-final-step.

45 With about four minutes . . . the [defensive] unit, pronto.": Rittenberg, "Spartans Feeling Rosy."

45 I'm like 'Oh, man, it's getting real. We've gotta step up.': Rittenberg, "Spartans Feeling Rosy."

46 "I like these goal-line stands . . . on a wet field anyway.: Rexrode, *Stadium Stories*, p. 62.

46 "I told [assistant coach] . . . 'Head Coach' in large letters.: Stabley, *The Spartans*, pp. 175-76.

46 The players "were so high . . . get them down for practice.: Stabley, *The Spartans*, p. 194.

46 "Imagine that. Lady Godiva . . . looking at white horses.: Stabley, *The Spartans*, p. 212.

46 "Football is not a contact . . . Dancing is a contact sport.": Stabley, *The Spartans*, p. 202.

46 "Remember, Duffy, we're with you win or tie.": Stabley, *The Spartans*, p. 206.

46 "Sherman Lewis is a . . . one weakness. He's a senior.": Stabley, *The Spartans*, p. 217.

46 We've learned our lesson. . . . anyone that smart again.: Stabley, *The Spartans*, p. 227.

47 assistant coach Tarz Taylor had a . . . give to some friends.: Stabley, *The Spartans*, pp. 65-66.

47 The local police told . . . on the Red Cedar River: Stabley, *The Spartans*, p. 66.

47 One sales in those days . . . the game at the gate.: Stabley, *The Spartans*, p. 66.

48 In East Lansing for the . . . shout at one another.: Dana O'Neil, "The Steps That Led Tom Izzo to the Doors," *ESPN.com*, Sept. 8, 2016, http://www.espn.com/mens-college-basketball/story_/id_17485035/the-10-steps-led-michigan-state-coach-tom-izzo-hall-fame.

48 I figured with his . . . he deserved something.: O'Neil, "The Steps That Led Tom Izzo."

49 Enos was not a . . . make a Big Ten player.: Henning, *Spartan Seasons II*, p. 14.

49 Offensive coordinator Morris Watts . . . him than for him.: Henning, *Spartan Seasons II*, p. 15.

49 He established a routine . . . being a line coach.: Henning, *Spartan Seasons II*, p. 16.

49 Here was a kid whose . . . a starting quarterback.: Henning, *Spartan Seasons II*, p. 16.

50 "The most physical team on the West Coast": Bruce Feldman, "Rose Bowl: Former Walk-On Kyler Elsworth Hero for Michigan State," *CBSSports*, Jan. 1, 2014, http://www.cbssports.com/college-football/news/rose-bowl-former-walk-on-kyler-elsworth-hero-for-michigan-state/.

50 "Once I saw their offensive . . . to go over the top,": Feldman, "Rose Bowl."

50 [Kyler] Elsworth [was] the . . . a fill-in for an accomplished defense.: Stephen Brooks, "Kyler Elsworth Seals MSU's Rose Bowl Victory," in *Reaching Higher*, p. 78.

51 During his senior year . . . let alone play football.: Brad Biggs, "Arthur Ray Jr. an Uplifting Story," *Chicago Tribune*, March 3, 2015, http://www.chicagotribune.com/sports/football/bears/ct-biggs-nfl-spt-0304-20150303-story.html.

51 Ray endured nine surgeries, . . . he couldn't walk without crutches.: "Arthur Ray Wins Courage Award," *ESPN.com*, Dec. 19, 2011, http://www.espn.com/college-football/story/_/id/7369406/arthur-ray-michigan-state-spartans-lauded. courage.

51 "I'm walking through the . . . pass with slide protection,": Biggs, "Arthur Ray Jr."

51 I couldn't have a bad day. Those kids meant too much to me.: Biggs, "Arthur Ray Jr."

52 the night Earvin Johnson came "back from the 'dead.'": Stabley, Jr., and Staudt, *Tales of the Magical Spartans*, p. 58.

52 Jenison Field House held its . . . a period of time,": Stabley, Jr., and Staudt, *Tales of the Magical Spartans*, p. 58.

52 Johnson flatly told the doctor . . . for a trial run.: Stabley, Jr., and Staudt, *Tales of the Magical Spartans*, p. 58.

52 "Earvin did enough for us . . . Johnson was good to go.: Stabley, Jr., and Staudt, *Tales of the Magical Spartans*, p. 59.

52 They'd already made up their . . . there was no tomorrow.: Stabley, Jr., and Staudt, *Tales of the Magical Spartans*, p. 58.

53 a small rural town with . . . green-and-white hearing aids.: Dan Murphy, "How 13-Year-Old Barak Price Became an Inspiration for the Spartans," *ESPN.com*, Nov. 6, 2015, http://www.espn.com/college-football-story/_/id/14057178/josiah-price-michigan-state-spartans-draw-inspiration-13-year-old-barak-price.

54 A couple of weeks into . . . Daugherty to join him.: Duffy Daugherty with Dave Diles, *Duffy* (Garden City, NY: Doubleday & Company, Inc., 1974), p. 15.

54 When one of the . . . most anything he likes.": Daugherty with Diles, *Duffy*, p. 16.

55 That outburst sent Spartan sports . . . until you get [the record].": Stabley, *The Spartans*, p. 254.

MICHIGAN STATE

55 Not Red Grange . . . better game than [Allen's].: Stabley, *The Spartans*, p. 253.

56 "I used to get really . . . became a team leader.: "Guard Leads Team into Elite Eight," *ESPN.com*, March 29, 2005, http://www.espn.com/ncw/ncaatourney05/news/story?id=2024054.

56 My sophomore year I was drained all the time.: "Guard Leads Team into Elite Eight."

57 He left in his wake . . . part of the Perles regime.": Henning, *Spartan Seasons II*, p. 105.

57 especially after impressing McPherson . . . to be State's head coach.: Henning, *Spartan Seasons II*, p. 113.

57 One was so bad . . . all the current assistants.: Henning, *Spartan Seasons II*, pp. 108-09.

57 He showed up more . . . or his club sandwich.: Henning, *Spartan Seasons II*, pp. 113-14.

57 Saban flew back to . . . had nailed the interview.: Henning, *Spartan Seasons II*, p. 114.

58 He called his former mentor . . . trouble seeing the difference. Josh Moyer, "Evolution of Michigan's State Tony Lippett," *ESPN.com*, Oct. 30, 2014, http://www.espn.com/blog/bigten/post/_/id/110103/evolution-of-michigan-states-tony-lippett.

58 [The advice] forced me . . . looking at everybody else.: Moyer, "Evolution."

59 "with some of the most . . . in all of college football.": Adam Rittenberg, "Spartans Blended Race in 1960s," *ESPN.com*, Feb. 21, 2013, http://www.espn.com/college-football/story/_/id/8970293/segregation-led-star-players-michigan-state-spartans-1960s-college-football.

59 "If they could have . . . white swimmers from Indiana.: Rittenberg, "Spartans Blended Race in 1960s."

59 Everything was completely segregated . . . a great, great welcoming.: Rittenberg, "Spartans Blended Race in 1960s."

60 "It was basketball one through . . . wouldn't have had the grades.": Dana O'Neil, "Day-Day's Journey to East Lansing," *ESPN.com*, Feb. 28, 2012, http://www.espn.com/mens-college-basketball/story/_/id/7621520/love-affair-michigan-state-spartans-started-early-draymond-green-college-basketball.

60 On his own, [Draymond . . . she'd done for him.: O'Neil, "Day-Day's Journey."

61 Chester Brewer wrought an athletic miracle.": Stabley, *The Spartans, p.* 19.

61 In 1903, he took over . . . immediately revolutionized it.": Stabley, *The Spartans* p. 19.

61 Brewer "put together the . . . the tiny farmer's college: Stabley, *The Spartans*, p. 19.

61 He "completely won over . . . Financial problems abated.: Stabley, *The Spartans*, p. 19.

61 He made a determined . . . tie with Michigan in 1908.: Stabley, *The Spartans*, p. 21.

61 Players were carried from . . . Lansing in celebration.: Stabley, *The Spartans*, p. 22.

61 "Brewer was simply the . . . ever happened to MAC.": Stabley, *The Spartans*, p. 26.

61 No man did more . . . compatible with higher education.: Stabley, *The Spartans*, p. 21.

62 Keith Nichol stood patiently waiting to see where the ball would fall.: Michelle Martinelli, "A Hail of a Win," in *Reaching Higher*, p. 58.

62 a "last-ditch jump ball . . . "That usually doesn't happen.": Kevin Allen, "Michigan State Stuns Wisconsin with Score on Final Play," *USA Today*, Oct. 23, 2011, http://usatoday30.usa today.com/sports/college/football/bigten/story2011-10-22/michigan-state-wisconsin/508728161/.

62 senior wide receiver B.J. Cunningham . . . to see what happened.: Michelle Martinelli, "A Hail of a Win," in *Reaching Higher*, p. 58.

62 the defender in the prime . . . mistimed his leap.: Sean Yuille, "Michigan State vs. Wisconsin Final Score," *SBNation.com*, Oct. 23, 2011. http://detroit.sbnation.com/michigan-st-spartans/2011-10-23/2507695/wisconsin-vs-michigan-state-score-recap-2011.

62 It bounced off Cunningham's face mask: Michelle Martinelli, "A Hail of a Win," in *Reaching Higher*, p. 58.

62 "He used all of his . . . power into the end zone.": Allen, "Michigan State Stuns Wisconsin."

62 A Hail Mary with no . . . longer is pretty dramatic.: SpartanDan, "Revisiting Michigan State Football's Most Memorable Endings," *TheOnlyColors.com*, Oct. 20, 2015, http://www.the onlycolors.com/2015/10/20/9572331/michigan-state-footballs-most-memorable-endings.

63 Prior to the 2016 season, . . . Kick Returner: DeAndra'Cobb.: Brian Bennett, "Michigan State's 'All-Century' Team," *ESPN.com*, July 13, 2016, http://www.espn.com/blog/bigten/post/_/id/134395/michigan-states-all-century-team-best-lineup-since-2000.

63 This is the top . . . have played since 2000.: Bennett, "Michigan State's 'All-Century' Team."

64 "We can slow it down, get offensive rebounds and hurt people,": Alexander Wolff, "State of Siege," *Sports Illustrated*, April 10, 2000, http:www.si.com/vault/2000/04/10/278133/state-of-siege.

64 The Spartans "seemed to . . . into prehistory with them,": Wolff, "State of Siege."

SPARTANS

64   The first team to 40 . . . would crack that mark.: Wolff, "State of Siege."
64   Michigan State's fourth meeting . . . breeds contemptible basketball.: Wolff, "State of Siege."
65   The Bullough family has been . . . of Football" at Michigan State.: Mick McCabe, "A Bullough Could Lead Michigan State," *Detroit Free Press*, July 30, 2016, http://www.freep.com/ story/sports/college/michigan-state/spartans/2016/07/30/michigan-state-spartans-riley-bullough/87839596/.
65   Her grandfather, Jim Morse, . . . competitive of the four.: Scott DeCamp, "Michigan State in Bullough Siblings' Blood," *MLive.com*, Sept. 15, 2016, http://www.mlive.com/spartans/ index.ssf/2016/09/bullough_name_synonymous_with.html.
65   at times the home . . . over at that house?": DeCamp, "Michigan State in Bullough Siblings' Blood."
65   As you can see, . . . athletes in this family.: DeCamp, "Michigan State in Bullough Siblings' Blood."
66   "one of the least . . . most celebrated sports figure.": Rexrode, *Spartan Stories*, p. 104.
66   In the fall of 1974, . . . teammates from day one.: Rexrode, *Spartan Stories*, p. 104.
66   He :tried baseball on a whim": Rexrode, *Spartan Stories*, p. 109.
66   All this from a guy nobody recruited.: Rexrode, *Spartan Stories*, p. 106.
67   "NO. 1 VS. NO ONE." . . . State game of Oct 13, 1990.: Rexrode, *Spartan Stories*, p. 148.
67   "It didn't really make . . .were a powerhouse team, too.": Rexrode, *Spartan Stories*, p. 148.
67   "When I got past him, . . . him away, he fell.": Rexrode, *Spartan Stories*, p. 152.
67   "You guys saw it. It was ridiculous.": Rexrode, *Spartan Stories*, p. 153.
67   They have an argument.: Rexrode, *Spartan Stories*, p. 153.
68   So many students made . . . by train in history.": Stabley, *The Spartans*, p. 181.
68   The weather was clear . . . Rose Bowl games ever.: Stabley, *The Spartans*, p. 184.
68   his first-ever field goal: Stabley, *The Spartans*, p. 179.
68   Kaiser was in the middle . . . swung through again.: Stabley, *The Spartans*, p. 179.
68   A story-book finish that . . . duplicated with a script.: Stabley, *The Spartans*, p. 191.
69   In Huffman's first few seconds . . . get the shoe on properly.: Stabley, Jr., and Staudt, *Tales of the Magical Spartans*, p. 71.
69   NBC commentator Al McGuire noticed . . . start calling him "Shorts.": Stabley, Jr., and Staudt, *Tales of the Magical Spartans*, p. 72.
69   When I got to the floor, . . . That was pretty incredible.: Stabley, Jr., and Staudt, *Tales of the Magical Spartans*, p. 72.
70   The only Big Ten school . . . come to East Lansing.: Jeremy Warnemuende, "Leaving a Legacy," in *Reaching Higher*, p. 51.
70   "I remember talking to . . . and make a play?'": Warnemuende, "Leaving a Legacy," in *Reaching Higher*, p. 51.
70   As he prepared to run . . . 'Oh, yeah, yeah,": Warnemuende, "Leaving a Legacy," in *Reaching Higher*, p. 51.
70   Dantonio and Jones' position . . . they came to see.: Warnemuende, "Leaving a Legacy," in *Reaching Higher*, p. 53.
70   When I first came here, . . . just want an opportunity.: Warnemuende, "Leaving a Legacy," in *Reaching Higher*, p. 51.
71   We make a lot of people look foolish.": "Michigan State Ends Ohio State's 23-Game Win Streak," *ESPN.com*, Nov. 22, 2015, http://cdn.espn.com/ncf/recap?gameId=400763573.
71   "We came in with something . . . and play a little harder.: "Michigan State Ends Ohio State's 23-Game Win Streak."
71   The Spartans relish the role of underdog like no powerhouse program.: "Michigan State Ends Ohio State's 23-Game Win Streak."
72   College players often played . . . received $150 plus expenses.: Stabley, *The Spartans*, p. 60.
72   I never could have finished school otherwise.: Stabley, *The Spartans*, p. 61.
72   "a lovable roly-poly . . . master at public relations: Stabley, *The Spartans*, p. 58.
72   Young joined with the . . . every sport but football.: Stabley, *The Spartans*, p. 61.
72   A defeat of Michigan . . . lawnmover," the school's first.: Stabley, *The Spartans*, p. 62.
72   The police had to . . . passersby with rotten eggs.: Stabley, *The Spartans*, p. 63.
72   [Football players] switched freely from school to school.: Stabley, *The Spartans*, p. 60.
73   When *ESPN* called coach . . . of the USS Carl Vinson.: Andy Katz, "Spartans, Huskies to Tip Off in Germany," *ESPN.com*, Nov. 7, 2012, http://www.espn.com/ mens-college-basketball/blog/_.names/katz_andy/id/8603396/tom-izzo-

michigan-state-spartans-look-forward-another-opportunity-play-overseas-military-base.

73   After landing in Germany on . . . is the ultimate sacrifice.": Andy Katz, "Day 1 in Germany Has Sobering Effect," *ESPN.com*, Nov. 8, 2012, http://www.espn.com/mens-college-basketball/blog/_/name/katz_andy/id/8606841/day-1-germany-sobering-effect-michigan-state-spartans-uconn-huskies-college-basketball.

73   It's tough to leave this team here. I'm disappointed.: Katz, "Day 1 in Germany."

74   Football teams of the time . . . and counter the formation.: Stabley, *The Spartans*, pp. 91-92.

74   He gave each of the . . . backs had been identified.: Stabley, *The Spartans*, p. 92.

74   Despite trailing 7-0, he . . . reserves in the second half.: Stabley, *The Spartans*, p. 92.

74   Sid Wagner walk[ed] up . . . in complete amazement.: Stabley, *The Spartans*, p. 92.

75   "We didn't finish our . . . 20 to 25-plus points,": "Michigan State's D Toys with Ohio State," *ESPN.com*, Oct. 1, 2011, http://www.espn.com/ncf/recap?gameId=312740194.

75   The Buckeyes "were a complete mess": Brian Bennett, "Michigan State Knocks Out Ohio State," *ESPN.com*, Oct. 1, 2011, http://www.espn.com/blog/bigten/post/_/id/34524/michigan-state-knocks-out-ohio-state.

75   raining down a hearty chorus of boos: "Michigan State's D Toys with Ohio State."

75   The Spartans should have . . . comfortable final score.: Bennett, "Michigan State Knocks Out."

76   the players launched an . . . Williams had his meeting.: Henning, *Spartan Seasons* II, p. 172.

76   One overriding theme . . . assistant coaches stay, too..: Henning, *Spartan Seasons* II, p. 174.

76   dead center even. . . . never saw the game winner.: Henning, *Spartan Seasons* II, p. 181.

76   [The players] made a . . . above the crossbar.: Henning, *Spartan Seasons* II, p. 181.

77   For Litwhiler, an essential . . . players in a bed.: Henning, Spartan Seasons, p. 239.

77   A Lansing auto dealer arranged . . . benefits for the program.: Henning, *Spartan Seasons*, p. 240.

77   The usual format for . . . the host school's student union.: Henning, *Spartan Seasons*, p. 241.

77   The baseball team's Florida trip was an exercise in austerity.: Henning, *Spartan Seasons*, p. 239.

78   After the game, the MAC . . . jubilantly sang their fight song.: "The MSU Fight Song," *SpartanBand.net*, http://spartanband.net/history/early-1900s/.

78   An accomplished pianist and . . . song for the college.: "The MSU Fight Song."

78   In 1919, Lankey was an . . . Fight Song was a winner.": "Traditions: MSU Fight Song," *MSU Spartans.net*, http://www.msuspartans.net/trads/msu-traditions.html.

79   "That's the rule rather . . . the hair had to go: Dan Murphy, "Evan Jones Ready for 'His Time,'" *ESPN.com*, April 20, 2016, http://www.espn.com/blog/bigten/post/_/id/132389/evan-jones-ready-for-his-time-on-msus-defensive-line.

79   It was a good decision for sure.: Murphy, "Evan Jones Ready for 'His Time.'"

80   He prevailed upon a . . . returned the boat pronto.: Stabley, *The Spartans*, pp. 34-35.

80   When [Gladys Olds] finished, . . . and in good condition.: Stabley, *The Spartans*, p. 35.

81   The Hawkeyes called two . . . there was dead silence.": Stabley, Jr. and Staudt, *Tales of the Magical Spartans*, p. 54.

82   "wiry kid with blond . . . the Menace about him": Henning, *Spartan Seasons* II, p. 9.

82   When head coach George . . . vacation to Las Vegas.: Henning, *Spartan Seasons* II, pp. 9-10.

82   A Pittsburgh native . . . one-word scouting report: "Wow.": Henning, *Spartan Seasons* II, p. 10.

83   Malik McDowell's fourth-down . . . five defenders against Iowa: Dan Murphy, "10 Plays that Landed Michigan State in the College Football Playoff," *ESPN.com*, Dec. 24, 2015, http://www.espn.com/blog/bigten/post/_/id/128850/ten-plays-that-landed-michigan-state-in-the-college-football-playoff.

84   A field goal was problematical . . . on the far hash.: Adam Rittenberg, "Mark Dantonio's Faith Drives Special Season," *ESPN.com*, Oct. 23, 2010, http://www.espn.com/blog/bigten/post/_/id/18462/dantonios-faith-drives-msus-special-season.

84   To have a special . . . roll the dice at times.: Rittenberg, "Mark Dantonio's Faith."

85   Head coach Tom Izzo made . . . because of various injuries.: Dana O'Neil, "Travis Trice's Road to Indianapolis," *ESPN.com*, March 29, 2015, http://www.espn.com/mens-college-basketball/tournament/2015/story/_/id/12583327/michigan-state-spartans-travis-trice-completes-long-road-final-four-win-louisville-cardinals.

85   "a skinny, undersized . . . as his faith deepened.: O'Neil, "Travis Trice's Road."

85   As strangely as [Trice's] . . . a man of deep faith.: O'Neil, "Travis Trice's Road."

86   the first athletic equipment . . . and eight ducks.: Lyman L. Frimodig and Fred W. Stabley, *Spartan Saga* (Michigan State University: East Lansing, 1971), p. 7.

86   The students started the . . . from the student body.: Frimodig and Stabley, p. 27.

86 A squad in 1884 didn't . . . having its picture taken.": Frimodig and Stabley, p. 35.
86 Basketball was played in . . . that played indoor polo.: Frimodig and Stabley, p. 75.
86 In 1871, a MAC baseball . . . [had to] hitch-hike home.: Frimodig and Stabley, p. 7.
87 Charles "Bubba Smith knew . . . named his starting defense.: Rexrode, *Stadium Stories*, p. 51.
87 The defensive starters included . . . teams were all white: Rexrode, *Stadium Stories*, p. 52.
87 Even colleges that had . . . money and fan support.: Rexrode, *Stadium Stories*, p. 54.
87 with ten starters on . . . that unwritten racist rule.: Rexrode, *Stadium Stories*, p. 52.
87 Duffy [Daugherty] took a . . . the other black players.: Rexrode, *Stadium Stories*, p. 54.
88 "Hidden beneath his fierce . . . name hadn't been called.: Jacob Carpenter, "Three of a Kind," in
      Reaching Higher, p. 33.
88 "maturity and loyalty of a . . . an elementary school carnival.: Carpenter, "Three of a Kind," in
      Reaching Higher, p. 31.
88 For the adult [Javon Ringer], it's about providing for family and honoring God.: Carpenter,
      "Three of a Kind," in *Reaching Higher*, p. 33.
89 "the greatest non-recruit in . . . Green ever played a game.: Jack Ebling, "Johnny Green: The
      Ultimate Walk-On," *MSUSpartans.com*, Feb. 24, 2009, http://www.msuspartans.com/
      genrel/022409aac.html.
89 despicable, vile, unprincipled scoundrels.": John MacArthur, *Twelve Ordinary Men* (Nashville:
      W Publishing Group, 2002), p. 152.
89 Find out what this guy needs and get it to him, no matter what.: Ebling, "Johnny Green."
90 "You know it was funny," . . . let ourselves get down.": Geoff Preston, "MSU Comes Back to
      Win the Cotton Bowl, 'Never Lost Belief,'" in *Reaching Higher*, p. 92.
90 "triggering a Green and White frenzy": Ben Phlegar, "Dantonio Reflects on Dramatic
      Cotton Bowl Comeback," *MSUSpartans.com*, Jan. 6, 2015, http://www.msuspartans.
      com/sports/m-footbl/spec-rel/010615aae.html.
90 We had a belief that we could come back.": Steve Grinczel, "Spartans Rally from 20-Point
      Deficit, Win Cotton Bowl," *MSUSpartans.com*, Jan. 1, 2015, http://www.msuspartans.com/
      sports/m-footbl/spec-rel/010115aab.html.
90 I never lost belief. I never doubted myself or our team.: Preston, "MSU Comes Back," in
      Reaching Higher, p. 94.
91 Munn was convinced Crisler . . . to embarrass him.: Rexrode, *Stadium Stories*, p. 36.
91 Crisler kept his starters in for the full 60 minutes: Stabley, *The Spartans*, p. 121.
91 As the team prepared . . . door and dry safety.: Rexrode, *Stadium Stories*, p. 33.
91 They arrived on the . . . pipe must have cracked.: Rexrode, *Stadiuim Stories*, p. 39.
91 He was so downcast . . . into the dressing room.: Stabley, *The Spartans*, p. 122.
91 "We didn't think it was accidental, let's put it that way.: Rexrode, *Stadium Stories*, p. 39.
92 "an anemic 227" of them: Jen Neale, "2012 Buffalo Wild Wings Bowl Results," *SBNation.com*,
      Dec. 30, 2012, http://www.sbnation.com/2012/12/30/3816586/tcu-michigan-state-2012-
      buffalo-wild-wing-bowl-final-score.
92 "a little bit of fumbles luck.": "Bill Connelly, Saturday College Football Bowl Recaps," *SBNation.
      com*, Dec. 30, 2012, http://www.sbnation.com/college-football/2012/12/30/3817128/college-
      bowl-games-texas-football-alamo-bowl.
92 It won [State] the game.: Connelly, "Saturday College Football Bowl Recaps."
93 from the Gators' all-court . . . "Who's going to step up?": Wolff, "State of Siege."
93 Bell moved to the . . . Florida was already broken.": Wolff, "State of Siege."
93 I dropped a couple . . . me out of this one.: Wolff, "State of Siege."
94 "the most glorious achievement in Michigan State athletic history": Stabley, *The Spartans*,
      p. 156.
94 At a movie studio, . . . hitting some night spots.: Stabley, *The Spartans*, p. 160.
94 The squad was so small . . . called them "midgets.": Stabley, *The Spartans*, p. 159.
94 Various team members were . . . to cover their heads.: Stabley, *The Spartans*, pp. 160-61.
94 They had the fire under . . . of stairs to safety.: Stabley, *The Spartans*, p. 161.
94 These young men prevented . . . of life and property.: Stabley, *The Spartans*, p. 161.
95 averaging only 14.4 points . . . out of 127 teams.: Tom Shanahan, "Duffy Called QB Option,"
      Shanahan Report, Nov. 3, 2014, http://shanahan.report/a/duffy-called-qb-option-for-
      final-upset-of-ohio-state-in-1972.
95 after the 1-2 start in '72, . . . their head coach and to Krijt.: Shanahan, "Duffy
      Called QB Option."
95 This has to rate very high on my list.: Shanahan, "Duffy Called QB Option."

WORKS CITED

"2001 Michigan vs. Michigan State Football Game." *Wikipedia, the free encyclopedia.* https://en. wikipedia.org/wiki/2001_Michigan_vs_Michigan_State_football_game.

"2016 Auditions." *SpartanBand.net.* 23 Jan. 2016. http://spartanband.net/2016-auditions/.

Allen, Kevin. "Michigan State Stuns Wisconsin with Score on Last Play." *USA Today.* 23 Oct. 2011. http://usatoday30.usatoday.com/sports/college/football/bigten/story/2011-10-22/ michigan-state-wisconsin/50872816/.

"Arthur Ray Wins Courage Award." *ESPN.com.* 19 Dec. 2011. http://www.espn.com/college-football/story/_/id/7369406/arthur-ray-michigan-state-spartans-lauded. courage.

Austin, Kyle. "Led by Lorenzo White's 56-Carry Day, Spartans Have Put Up Big Numbers Against Indiana." *MLive.com.* 17 Oct. 2014. http://www.mlive.com/spartans/index-ssf/2014/10/led_by_lorenzo_whites_56-carry.html.

Bao, Robert. "The MSU Songs: Smashing Through the Myths." *Michigan State University Alumni Magazine.* 26 Aug. 2013. alumni.msu.edu/newsarticle.cfmid=573.

Bennett, Brian. "Brady Hoke Apologizes for Stake." *ESPN.com.* 26 Oct. 2014. http://www.espn.com/ college-football/story/_/id/11767910/brady-hoke-apologizes-michigan-state.

-----. "Michigan State Knocks Out Ohio State." *ESPN.com.* 1 Oct. 2011. http://www.espn.com/blog/ bigten/post/_/id/34524/michigan-state-knocks-out-ohio-state.

-----. "Michigan State's 'All-Century' Team: Best Lineup since 2000." *ESPN.com.* 13 July 2016. http://www.espn.com/blog/bigten/post/_/id/134395/michigan-states-all-century-team-best-lineup-since-2000.

-----. "Wisconsin Win Had Dantonio Dancing." *ESPN.com.* 30 Oct. 2012. http://www. espn.com/ blog/bigten/post/_/id/63796/wisconsin-win-had-dantonio-dancing.

Biggers, Adam. "Amp Campbell Will Always Be a Michigan State Spartan." *BleacherReport.com.* 22 Aug. 2010. http://bleacherreport.com/articles/441193-amp-campbell-will-always-be-a-michigan-state-spartan#.

Biggs, Brad. "Arthur Ray Jr. an Uplifting Story at Northwestern Pro Day." *Chicago Tribune.* 3 March 2015. http://www.chicagotribune.com/sports/football/bears/ct-biggs-nfl-spt-0304-20150303-story.html.

Calloway, Brian. "Big Heart Fuels Tori Jankoska in Record-Setting MSU Career." *Lansing State Journal.* 13 Feb. 2017. http://www.lansingstatejournal.com/story/sports/college/msu-womens-basketball/2017/02/13/big-heart-fuels-tori-jankoska-record-setting-msu-career/97839870/.

-----. "Michigan State Player Helps Save Teenager's Life." *USA Today.* 5 Aug, 2013. http://www. usatoday.com/story/sports/ncaaf/bigten/2013/08/05/michigan-state-micajah-reynolds-helps-save-teenagers-life/2621903/.

Connelly, Bill. "Saturday College Football Bowl Recaps: Comebacks Are Fun and So Is Near-Perfection." *SB Nation.com.* 30 Dec. 2012. http://www.sbnation.com/college-foot-ball/2012/12/30/3817128/college-bowl-games-texas-football-alamo-bowl.

Couch, Graham. "Injury at Oregon Altered Amp Campbell's Life." *Lansing State Journal.* 5 Sept. 2014. http://www.lansingstatejournal.com/story/sports/columnists/graham-couch/2014/09/05/injury-oregon-altered-amp-campbells-life/15109817/.

-----. "MSU's Top 50 Basketball Players: No. 6 Greg Kelser." *Lansing State Journal.* 12 Sept. 2014. http://www.lansingstatejournal.com/story/sports/college/msu/couchonfire/2014/09/ 12/msu-top-50-greg-kelser/15506721/.

-----. "MSU's Top 50 Football Players: No. 9 Brad Van Pelt." *Lansing State Journal.* 30 July 2015. http://www.lansingstatejournal.com/story/sports/college/msu/top50-football/2015/ 07/29/msu-top-50-brad-van-pelt-30842845/.

Daugherty, Duffy with Dave Diles. *Duffy: An Autobiography.* Garden City, NY: Doubleday & Company, Inc., 1974.

DeCamp, Scott. "Michigan State in Bullough Siblings' Blood, But Don't Forget Morse/Notre Dame Ties." *MLive.com.* 15 Sept. 2016. http://www.mlive.com/spartans/index.ssf/2016/09/ bullough_name_synonymous_with.html.

Ebling, Jack. "Johnny Green: The Ultimate Walk-On." *MSUSpartans.com.* 24 Feb. 2009. http://www. msusports.com/genrel/022409aac.html.

SPARTANS

Feldman, Bruce. "Rose Bowl: Former Walk-On Kyler Elsworth Hero for Michigan State." *CBS Sports*. 1 Jan. 2014. http://www.cbssports.com/college-football/news/rose-bowl-former-walk-on-kyler-elsworth-hero-for-michigan-state/.

"First Band Formed in 1870." *SpartanBand.net*. http://spartanband.net/history/origins/.

Fortuna, Matt. "Calhoun's Dual Role: Hit 'Em, Make 'Em Smile." *ESPN.com*. 29 Aug. 2014. http://www.espn.com/blog/bigten/post_/id/106258/calhoun-still-improving-on-and-off-the-field.

Frimodig, Lyman L. and Fred W. Stabley. *Spartan Saga: A History of Michigan State Athletics*. Michigan State University: East Lansing, 1971.

"Gerald Holmes." *MSUSpartans.com*, www.msuspartans.com/sports/m-footbl/mtt/gerald_holmes_855512.html.

Grinczel, Steve. "Brad Van Pelt Was One of MSU's All-Time Greats." *MLive.com*. 19 Feb. 2009. http://www.mlive.com/spartans/index-ssf/2009-02/post_1.html.

-----. "Celebrating the Legacy of Gideon Smith." *MSUSpartans.com*. 15 Oct. 2013. www.msuspartans.com/sports/m-football/spec-rel-101513aae.html.

-----. "Spartans Rally from 20-Point Deficit, Win Cotton Bowl." *MSUSpartans.com*. 1 Jan. 2015. http://www.msuspartans.com/sports/m-footbl/spec-rel/010115aab.html.

"Guard Leads Team into Elite Eight." *ESPN.com*. 29 March 2005. http://www.espn.com/ncw/ncaa-tourney05/news/story?id=2024054.

Hays, Graham. "Jefferson Helps Sparty Stomach BGSU." *ESPN.com*. 20 March 2010. http://www.espn.com/ncw/tournament/2010/columns/story?id=5012998&columnist=hays_graham.

Henning, Lynn.: *Spartan Seasons: The Triumphs and Turmoil of Michigan State Sports*. Bloomfield Hills, Mich.: Momentum Publishing, 1987.

-----. *Spartan Seasons II: More Triumphs and Turmoil of Michigan State Sports*. Bloomfield Hills, Mich.: Sports Seasons Publishing LLC, 2006.

Katz, Andy. "Day 1 in Germany Has Sobering Effect." *ESPN.com*. 8 Nov. 2012. http://www.espn.com/mens-college-basketball/blog/_/name/katz_andy/id/8606841/day-1-germany-sobering-effect-michigan-state-spartans-uconn-huskies-college-basketball.

-----. "Spartans, Huskies to Tip Off in Germany." *ESPN.com*. 7 Nov. 2012. http://www.espn.com/mens-college-basketball/blog/_.names/katz_andy/id/8603396/tom-izzo-michigan-state-spartans-look-forward-another-opportunity-play-overseas-military-base-college-basketball.

Layden, Tim. "Altered State." *Sports Illustrated*. 18 Oct. 1999. http://www.si.com/vault/1999/10/18/268360/altered-state-as-michigan-learned-the-hard-way.

Low, Chris. "'I'm at a Loss for Words' — The Sideline View of Michigan State's Miracle Win." *ESPN.com*. 19 Oct. 2015. http://cdn.espn.com/blog/bigten/post/_/id/125417/im-at-a-loss-for-words-the-sideline-view-of-michigan-states-miracle-win.

MacArthur, John. *Twelve Ordinary Men*. Nashville: W Publishing Group, 2002.

McCabe, Mick. "A Bullough Could Lead Michigan State in Tackles for Eighth Time." *Detroit Free Press*. 30 July 2016. http://www.freep.com/story/sports/college/michigan-state/spartans/2016/07/30/michigan-state-spartans-riley-bullough/87839596/.

McGee, Ryan. "The Bottom 10: Michigan Picks the Wrong Team to Mess With." *ESPN.com*. 29 Oct. 2014. http://www.espn.com/college-football/story/_/page/bottom102821/michigan-wolverines-mess-michigan-state-spartans.

"Michigan State Earns Share of Big Ten Title for First Time Since 1990." *ESPN.com*. 28 Nov. 2010. http://www.espn.com/ncf/recap/_/id/303310213.

"Michigan State Ends Ohio State's 23-Game Win Streak." *ESPN.com*. 22 Nov. 2015. http://cdn.espn.com/ncf/recap?gameId=400763573.

"Michigan State Stuns Michigan with Final-Play Fumble Return." *ESPN.com*. 17 Oct. 2015. http://cdn.espn.com/ncf/recap?gameId=400763542.

"Michigan State's D Toys with Ohio State, Rides 4th-Quarter FG to Win." *ESPN.com*. 1 Oct. 2011. http://www.espn.com/ncf/recap?gameId=312740194.

Moyer, Josh. "Evolution of Michigan's State Tony Lippett." *ESPN.com*. 30 Oct. 2014. http://www.espn.com/blog/bigten/post/_/id/110103/evolution-of-michigan-states-tony-lippett.

Murphy, Dan. "10 Plays that Landed Michigan State in the College Football

Playoff." *ESPN.com*. 24 Dec. 2015. http://www.espn.com/blog/bigten/post/_/id/128850/
ten-plays-that-landed-michigan-state-in-the-college-football-playoff.

-----. "Evan Jones Ready for 'His Time' on MSU's Defensive Line." *ESPN.com*. 20 April 2016. http://
www.espn.com/blog/bigten/post/_/id/132389/evan-jones-ready-for-his-time-on-
msus-defensive-line.

-----. "How 13-Year-Old Barak Price Became an Inspiration for the Spartans." *ESPN.com*. 6 Nov.
2015. http://www.espn.com/college-football-story/_/id/14057178/josiah-price-
michigan-state-spartans-draw-inspiration-13-year-old-barak-price.

-----. "MSU Irked by Wolverines' Slight." *ESPN.com*. 25 Oct. 2014. http://www.espn.com/college-
football/story/_/id/11764201/michigan-state-spartans-respond-perceived-slight-
michigan-wolverines.

-----. "Toughness Is a Family Trait for Michigan State's Allen Brothers." *ESPN.com*. 30 Dec. 2015.
http://www.espn.com/blog/bigten/post/_/id/129101/toughness-is-a-family-trait-for-
michigan-states-allen-brothers.

Neale, Jen. "2012 Buffalo Wild Wings Bowl Results: Spartans Come from 13 Down to Win 17-16
over TCU." *SBNation.com*. 30 Dec. 2012. http://www.sbnation.com/2012/12/30/
3816586/tcu-michigan-state-2012-buffalo-wild-wing-bowl-final-score.

"No. 5 Michigan State Wins Big Ten Championship over No. 4 Iowa, 16-13." *BigTen.org*. 5 Dec.
2015. http://www.bigten.org/sports/m-footbl/recaps/120515aaa.html.

O'Neil, Dana. "Day-Day's Journey to East Lansing." *ESPN.com*. 28 Feb. 2012. http://www.espn.
com/mens-college-basketball/story/_/id/7621520/love-affair-michigan-state-
spartans-started-early-draymond-green-college-basketball.

-----. "MSU's Valentine Next in Line of Spartan Leaders." *ESPN.com*. 9 Dec. 2015. http://www.espn.
com/mens-college-basketball/story/_/id/14320710/denzel-valentine-latest-long-line-
michigan-state-spartan-program-caretakers.

-----. "The Steps That Led Tom Izzo to the Doors of the Hall of Fame." *ESPN.com*. 8 Sept. 2016.
http://www.espn.com/mens-college-basketball/story/_/id_17485035/the-10-steps-led-
michigan-state-coach-tom-izzo-hall-fame.

-----. "Travis Trice's Road to Indianapolis." *ESPN.com*. 29 March 2015. http://www.espn.com/mens-
college-basketball/tournament/2015/story/_/id/12583327/michigan-state-spartans-
travis-trice-completes-long-road-final-four-win-louisville-cardinals.

Phlegar, Ben. "Dantonio Reflects on Dramatic Cotton Bowl Comeback." *MSUSpartans.com*. 6 Jan.
2015. http://www.msuspartans.com/sports/m-footbl/spec-rel/010615aae.html.

Reaching Higher: Mark Dantonio and the Rise of Michigan State Football. Chicago: Triumph Books
LLC, 2016.

"Report: Delany Says Officials Mistakenly Awarded TD to Michigan." *ESPN.com*. 27 Oct 2008.
http://www.espn.com/college-football/news/story?id=3666060.

Rexrode, Joe. *Stadium Stories: Michigan State Spartans*. Guilford, Conn.: The Globe Pequot Press,
2006.

Rittenberg, Adam. "Little Brother Takes Over the Big House." *ESPN.com*. 25 Oct. 2008. http://
www.espn.com/blog/bigten/post/_/id/878/little-brother-takes-over-the-big-house.

-----. "Mark Dantonio's Faith Drives Special Season." *ESPN.com*. 23 Oct. 2010. http://www.espn.
com/blog/bigten/post/_id/18462/dantonios-faith-drives-msus-special-season.

-----. "MSU's Conklin Makes Everyone Take Notice." *ESPN.com*. 16 June 2014. http://www.espn.
com/blog/bigten/post/_/id/102266/msus-conklin-making-everyone-take-notice.

-----. "Spartans Blended Race in 1960s." *ESPN.com*. 21 Feb. 2013. http://www.espn.com/college-
football/story/_/id/8970293/segregation-led-star-players-michigan-state-spartans-
1960s-college-football.

-----. "Spartans Feeling Rosy After Taking Final Step." *ESPN.com*. 8 Dec. 2013. http://www.espn.
com/blog/bigten/post/_/id/91192/spartans-feeling-rosy-after-taking-final-step.

-----. "Spartans Rally to Stun Wisconsin in OT." *ESPN.com*. 27 Oct. 2012. http://www.espn.com/
blog/bigten/post/_/id/63382/spartans-rally-to-stun-wisconsin-in-ot.

-----. "Spartans' Reynolds Helps Save Teen's Life." *ESPN.com*. 6 Aug. 2013. http://www.espn.com/
blog/bigten/post/_/id/80880/spartans-reynolds-helps-save-teens-life.

Ronberg, Gary. "Delicious Dessert for a Hungry Spartan Crew." *SI.com*. 3 April 1967. http://www.
si.com/vault/1967/04/03/608949/delicious-dessert-for-a-hungry-spartan-crew.

Schecter, B.J. "Turning the Corner: Michigan State's Amp Campbell Is No Ordinary Spartan, in More Ways Than One." *SI.com*. 13 Sept. 1999. http://www.si.com/vault/1999/09/13/8110447/turning-the-corner-michigan-states-amp-campbell-is-no-ordinary-spartan-in-more-ways-than-one.

Schlabach, Mark. "A Finish for the Ages at the Big House." *ESPN.com*. 18 Oct. 2015. http://cdn.espn.com/college-football/story/_/page/gamedayfinal101715/michigan-state-spartans-relish-win.

-----. "Kirk Cousins Used to Playing Long Odds." *ESPN.com*. 21 Oct. 2011. http://www.espn.com/college-football/story/_/id/7127370/michigan-state-quarterback-kirk-cousins-used-having-odds-stacked-him.

Schonbrun, Zach. "Shilique Calhoun Finds a Good Fit in Michigan State's Pass Rush." *The New York Times*. 15 Oct. 2015. http://www.nytimes.com/2015/10/16/sports/ncaafootball/michigan-state-shilique-calhoun-michigan-college-football.html?_r=o.

Shanahan, Tom. "Duffy Called QB Option for Final Upset of Ohio State in 1972." *Shanahan Report*. 3 Nov. 2014. http://shanahan.report/a/duffy-called-qb-option-for-final-upset-of-ohio-state-in-1972.

Solari, Chris. "1974 MSU-Ohio State Ending Still Bizarre 40 Years Later." *Lansing State Journal*. 1 Nov. 2014. http://www.lansingstatejournal.com/story/sports/college/msu/football/2014/11/01/msu-ohio-state-ending-still-bizarre-years-later/18352497/.

-----. "MSU's Gerald Holmes Overcomes Loss of Grandmother for 100 Yards, 2 TDs." *Lansing State Journal*. 18 Sept. 2016. http://www.lansingstatejournal.com/story/sports/college/msu/football/2016/09/18/msu-gerald-holmes-overcomes-loss-grandmother-100-yards-2-tds/90627724/.

-----. Spann, Denise, "Tori Jankoska Rises, Breaks Records During Final Season as a Spartan." *The State News*. 27 Feb. 2017. http://statenews.com/articles/2017/02/tori-jankoska-rises-breaks-records-during-final season-as-a-spartan.

SpartanDan. "Revisiting Michigan State Football's Most Memorable Endings." *TheOnlyColors.com*. 20 Oct. 2015. http://www.theonlycolors.com/2015/10/20/9572331/michigan-state-footballs-most-memorable-endings.

"Spartans Win at Big House for First Time Since 1990 Behind Ringer, Hoyer." *ESPN.com*. 25 Oct. 2008. http://www.espn.com/ncf/recap?gameId=282990130.

Stabley, Fred, Jr. and Tim Staudt. *Tales of the Magical Spartans*. Champaign, Ill.: Sports Publishing L.L.C., 2003.

Stabley, Fred W. *The Spartans: Michigan State Football*. Tomball, Texas: Strode Publishers, 2nd Edition, 1988.

"The MSU Fight Song." *SpartanBand.net*. http://spartanband.net/history/early-1900s/.

"Traditions: MSU Fight Song." *MSUSpartans.com*. http://www.msuspartans.com/trads/msu-traditions.html.

"Traditions: MSU Marching Band." *MSUSpartans.com*. http://www.msuspartans.com/trads/msu-traditions.html.

"Traditions: The Nickname." *MSUSpartans.com*. http://www.msuspartans.com/trads/msu-traditions.html.

Van Stratt, Gillian. "Michigan Versus Michigan State: Memorable Moments in the Battle for Backyard Bragging Rights." *Mlive.com*. 1 Nov. 2013. http://www.mlive.com/sports/index.ssf/2013/11/michigan_versus_michigan_state.html.

Wolff, Alexander. "State of Siege." *Sports Illustrated*. 10 April 2000. http:www.si.comvault/2000/04/10/278133/state-of-siege.

Yuille, Sean. "Michigan State vs. Wisconsin Final Score: Spartans Win on Last-Second Hail Mary, 37-31." *SBNation.com*. 23 Oct. 2011. http://detroit.sbnation.com/ michigan-st-spartans/2011/10/23/2507695/wisconsin-vs-michigan-state-score-recap-2011.

NAME INDEX
(LAST NAME, DEVOTION DAY NUMBER)

SCRIPTURES INDEX
(by DEVOTION DAY NUMBER)

SPARTANS

209